Our Human Rights

Editor: Tracy Biram

Volume 372

Independence Educational Publishers

First published by Independence Educational Publishers

The Studio, High Green

Great Shelford

Cambridge CB22 5EG

England

© Independence 2020

Copyright

Photocopy licence

ISBN-13: 978 1 86168 829 3

Printed in Great Britain

Zenith Print Group

Contents

Introduction

Our Human Rights is Volume 372 in the *ISSUES* series. The aim of the series is to offer current, diverse information about important issues in our world, from a UK perspective.

ABOUT OUR HUMAN RIGHTS

In spite of our ever socially evolving world, human rights violations around the globe continue to shock. In the ILO's (International Labour Organisation) latest report there are an estimated 40.3 million victims of human trafficking worldwide. In this book we look at the history of human rights, human rights law and human rights issues such as FGM, child marriage and modern slavery.

OUR SOURCES

Titles in the *ISSUES* series are designed to function as educational resource books, providing a balanced overview of a specific subject.

The information in our books is comprised of facts, articles and opinions from many different sources, including:

◆ Newspaper reports and opinion pieces

◆ Website factsheets

◆ Magazine and journal articles

◆ Statistics and surveys

◆ Government reports

◆ Literature from special interest groups.

A NOTE ON CRITICAL EVALUATION

Because the information reprinted here is from a number of different sources, readers should bear in mind the origin of the text and whether the source is likely to have a particular bias when presenting information (or when conducting their research). It is hoped that, as you read about the many aspects of the issues explored in this book, you will critically evaluate the information presented.

It is important that you decide whether you are being presented with facts or opinions. Does the writer give a biased or unbiased report? If an opinion is being expressed, do you agree with the writer? Is there potential bias to the 'facts' or statistics behind an article?

ASSIGNMENTS

In the back of this book, you will find a selection of assignments designed to help you engage with the articles you have been reading and to explore your own opinions. Some tasks will take longer than others and there is a mixture of design, writing and research-based activities that you can complete alone or in a group.

FURTHER RESEARCH

At the end of each article we have listed its source and a website that you can visit if you would like to conduct your own research. Please remember to critically evaluate any sources that you consult and consider whether the information you are viewing is accurate and unbiased.

Useful Websites

www.abouthumanrights.org.uk

www.actionaid.org.uk

www.amnesty.org.uk

www.equalityhumanrights.com

www.gov.uk

www.independent.co.uk

www.libertyhumanrights.org.uk

www.ohchr.org

www.stopthetraffik.org

www.telegraph.co.uk

www.theconversation.com

www.theferret.scot

www.theguardian.com

www.ukhumanrightsblog.com

www.weforum.org

What are human rights?

Human rights are rights inherent to all human beings, whatever our nationality, place of residence, sex, national or ethnic origin, colour, religion, language, or any other status. We are all equally entitled to our human rights without discrimination. These rights are all interrelated, interdependent and indivisible.

Universal human rights are often expressed and guaranteed by law, in the forms of treaties, customary international law, general principles and other sources of international law. International human rights law lays down obligations of Governments to act in certain ways or to refrain from certain acts, in order to promote and protect human rights and fundamental freedoms of individuals or groups.

Universal and inalienable

The principle of universality of human rights is the cornerstone of international human rights law. This principle, as first emphasized in the Universal Declaration on Human Rights in 1948, has been reiterated in numerous international human rights conventions, declarations, and resolutions. The 1993 Vienna World Conference on Human Rights, for example, noted that it is the duty of States to promote and protect all human rights and fundamental freedoms, regardless of their political, economic and cultural systems.

All States have ratified at least one, and 80% of States have ratified four or more, of the core human rights treaties, reflecting consent of States which creates legal obligations for them and giving concrete expression to universality. Some fundamental human rights norms enjoy universal protection by customary international law across all boundaries and civilizations.

Human rights are inalienable. They should not be taken away, except in specific situations and according to due process. For example, the right to liberty may be restricted if a person is found guilty of a crime by a court of law.

Interdependent and indivisible

All human rights are indivisible, whether they are civil and political rights, such as the right to life, equality before the law and freedom of expression; economic, social and cultural rights, such as the rights to work, social security and education; or collective rights, such as the rights to development and self-determination, are indivisible, interrelated and interdependent. The improvement of one right facilitates advancement of the others. Likewise, the deprivation of one right adversely affects the others.

Equal and non-discriminatory

Non-discrimination is a cross-cutting principle in international human rights law. The principle is present in all the major human rights treaties and provides the central theme of some of the international human rights conventions such as the International Convention on the Elimination of All Forms of Racial Discrimination and the Convention on the Elimination of All Forms of Discrimination against Women.

The principle applies to everyone in relation to all human rights and freedoms and it prohibits discrimination on the basis of a list of non-exhaustive categories such as sex, race, colour and so on. The principle of non-discrimination is complemented by the principle of equality, as stated in Article 1 of the Universal Declaration of Human Rights: "All human beings are born free and equal in dignity and rights."

Both rights and obligations

Human rights entail both rights and obligations. States assume obligations and duties under international law to respect, to protect and to fulfil human rights. The obligation to respect means that States must refrain from interfering with or curtailing the enjoyment of human rights. The obligation to protect requires States to protect individuals and groups against human rights abuses. The obligation to fulfil means that States must take positive action to facilitate the enjoyment of basic human rights. At the individual level, while we are entitled to our human rights, we should also respect the human rights of others.

2020

www.ohchr.org

A history of human rights in Britain

The idea that human beings should have a set of basic rights and freedoms has deep roots in Britain. Here are some of the national and international milestones that have shaped the concept of human rights in Britain over the last 800 years.

1215: the Magna Carta

This English Charter acknowledged for the first time that subjects of the crown had legal rights and that laws could apply to kings and queens too. The Magna Carta was also the first step in giving us the right to a trial by a jury of our peers.

1679: Habeas Corpus Act

Another crucial step towards the right to a fair trial, this law protected and extended the right of a detained person to go before a judge to determine whether the detention was legal.

1689: English Bill of Rights

The Bill was a landmark moment in the political history of Britain because it limited the powers of the monarch and set out the rights of Parliament. It included the freedom to petition the monarch (a step towards political protest rights); the freedom from cruel and unusual punishments (the forerunner to the ban on torture in our Human Rights Act) and the freedom from being fined without trial.

1948: Universal Declaration of Human Rights

The Universal Declaration of Human Rights is the foundation for modern human rights. After the Second World War, the international community recognised the need for a collective expression of human rights. Adopted by the General Assembly of the United Nations in 1948, the declaration sets out a range of rights and freedoms to which everyone, everywhere in the world, is entitled.

1950: the European Convention on Human Rights

Members of the Council of Europe used the Universal Declaration of Human Rights to draw up this treaty to secure basic rights both for their own citizens and for other nationalities within their borders. The Convention was signed in Rome in 1950, ratified by the UK in 1951 and came into force in 1953. Unlike the Universal Declaration, the European Convention on Human Rights contains rights which can be relied on in a court of law.

1965: Race Relations Act

This was the first legislation in the UK to address racial discrimination. Although it was criticised because it only covered discrimination in specified public places, the act laid the foundations for more effective legislation. It also set up the Race Relations Board to consider complaints brought under the act.

1965: International Convention on the Elimination of All Forms of Racial Discrimination

This was the first human rights treaty adopted by the United Nations (UN). The International Convention on the Elimination of All Forms of Racial Discrimination (CERD) defines what constitutes race discrimination and sets out a comprehensive framework for ensuring that civil, political, economic and social rights are enjoyed by all, without distinction of race, colour, descent or national or ethnic origin. The UK ratified CERD in 1969.

1966: UK signs up to the European Court of Human Rights

Six years after the European Court of Human Rights was created, the UK granted what is known as 'individual petition' - the right for people to take their cases directly to the court in Strasbourg.

1975: Sex Discrimination Act

The act made sex discrimination illegal in the areas of employment, education and the provision of goods, facilities and services.

1976: Race Relations Act

The Race Relations Act was established to prevent race discrimination. It made race discrimination unlawful in employment, training, housing, education and the provision of goods, facilities and services.

1976: International Covenant on Economic, Social and Cultural Rights (ICESCR)

The general principles expressed by the Universal Declaration of Human Rights were given specific legal force through these two covenants. The Universal Declaration of Human Rights, the International Covenant on Civil and Political Rights (ICCPR) and the International Covenant on Economic, Social and Cultural Rights (ICESCR) make up the International Bill of Rights.

"The arc of the moral universe is long, but it bends toward justice."
Martin Luther King, Jr.

1995: Disability Discrimination Act

This Act represented the first far-reaching legislation on discrimination against disabled people. It covered key areas of life such as employment and training, education, goods, facilities and services, premises and transport.

1998: Human Rights Act

In force since October 2000, the Human Rights Act incorporated into domestic law the rights and liberties enshrined in the European Convention on Human Rights. People in the UK no longer had to take complaints about human rights breaches to the European Court in Strasbourg – British courts could now hear these cases.

1979: Convention on the Elimination of All Forms of Discrimination against Women (CEDAW)

Often referred to as the 'bill of rights for women', the Convention on the Elimination of All Forms of Discrimination against Women defined what constitutes discrimination against women and sets out the core principles to protect their rights.

1984: UN Convention against Torture and Other Cruel, Inhuman or Degrading Treatment or Punishment

The most comprehensive international treaty dealing with torture, the Convention against Torture and Other Cruel, Inhuman or Degrading Treatment or Punishment became the first binding international instrument exclusively dedicated to preventing some of the most serious human rights violations of our time.

1989: UN Convention on the Rights of the Child

Governments worldwide promised all children the same rights by adopting the Convention on the Rights of the Child, also known as the CRC or UNCRC. The basic premise is that children (under the age of 18) are born with the same fundamental freedoms and inherent rights as all human beings, but with specific additional needs because of their vulnerability.

2006: Universal Periodic Review

The UN's new review system meant that, for the first time, the human rights records of all Member States would come under regular scrutiny through the Universal Periodic Review. It gave a clear message that all countries have scope to improve the way human rights are promoted and protected.

2008: UN Convention on the Rights of Persons with Disabilities (UNCRPD)

The UN Convention on the Rights of Persons with Disabilities (UNCRPD) was the first human rights treaty of the 21st Century. It reaffirms disabled people's human rights and signals a further major step in their journey to becoming full and equal citizens.

2010: the Equality Act

The Equality Act brought together more than 116 separate pieces of legislation into one single act - a new, streamlined legal framework to protect the rights of individuals and advance equality of opportunity for all.

9 October 2018

The Human Rights Act

What is the Human Rights Act?

The Human Rights Act is a UK law passed in 1998.

It lets you defend your rights in UK courts and compels public organisations – including the Government, police and local councils – to treat everyone equally, with fairness, dignity and respect.

Who can use the Human Rights Act?

The Human Rights Act may be used by every person resident in the UnitedKingdom regardless of whether or not they are a British citizen or a foreign national, a child or an adult, a prisoner or a member of the public.

It can even be used by companies or organisations (like Liberty).

What does the Human Rights Act actually do?

The human rights contained within this law are based on the articles of the European Convention on Human Rights.

The Act 'gives further effect' to rights and freedoms guaranteed under the European Convention. It means:

◆ Judges must read and give effect to other laws in a way which is compatible with Convention rights

◆ It is unlawful for a public authority to act in a way which is incompatible with a Convention right.

What rights does the Human Rights Act protect?

◆ The right to life: protects your life, by law. The State is required to investigate suspicious deaths and deaths in custody.

◆ The prohibition of torture and inhuman treatment: you should never be tortured or treated in an inhuman or degrading way, no matter what the situation.

◆ Protection against slavery and forced labour: you should not be treated like a slave or subjected to forced labour.

◆ The right to liberty and freedom: you have the right to be free and the State can only imprison you with very good reason – for example, if you are convicted of a crime.

◆ The right to a fair trial and no punishment without law: you are innocent until proven guilty. If accused of a crime, you have the right to hear the evidence against you in a court of law.

◆ Respect for privacy and family life and the right to marry: protects against unnecessary surveillance or intrusion into your life. You have the right to marry and enjoy family relationships.

◆ Freedom of thought, religion and belief: you can believe what you like and practise your religion or beliefs.

◆ Free speech and peaceful protest: you have a right to speak freely and join with others peacefully, to express your views.

◆ No discrimination: everyone's rights are equal. You should not be treated unfairly – because, for example, of your gender, race, disability, sexuality, religion or age.

◆ Protection of property: protects against state interference with your possessions.

◆ The right to an education: means that no child can be denied an education.

◆ The right to free elections: elections must be free and fair.

What does that mean for me?

If you can show that a public authority has interfered with any of the rights recognised by the Convention you can take action by:

◆ Writing to the public authority concerned to remind them of their legal obligations under the Human Rights Act and ask them to rectify the situation.

◆ Going to court, which may find that a particular action (or inaction) of a public authority is (or would be) unlawful. It can tell the public authority to stop interfering with your right or to take action to protect your right.

◆ If the court is satisfied that a law is incompatible with a Convention right, it may make a declaration of that incompatibility. This is a formal legal statement that the particular law interferes with human rights. It does not have immediate effect but strongly encourages Parliament to amend or repeal the law in question.

March 2020

Human rights and civil liberties

By Louise Smith, barrister

What are civil liberties?

The difference between human rights and civil liberties may be largely semantic. It could be said that human rights are those fundamental rights considered to be universal to all people. Civil liberties, however, may be those rights and freedoms recognised by a particular country.

Civil liberties are the rights and freedoms that protect an individual from the state and which are underpinned by a country's legal system. Civil liberties are the basic freedoms granted to a country's citizens – they are often defined by law (including, but not limited to, human rights law) and evidenced in government documentation. People need not earn civil rights - citizenship automatically confers them in most cases. Civil liberties prevent governments from abusing their powers and restrict the level of interference in people's lives.

Countries around the world may define civil liberties differently – and may, depending on prevailing circumstances, be more or less likely to uphold those civil liberties. This may be as true of notorious authoritarian states, as of countries which are celebrated for the permissive stance they take towards their citizens.

Where do civil liberties come from?

In 1215, King John of England signed the Magna Carta. At the time, John's principle motivation for signing the Magna Carta was to placate the medieval barons who were rebelling against the supreme power of the throne. Today it is considered by many people to be the blueprint for constitutions and bills of rights all over the world. The Magna Carta guaranteed certain basic levels of treatment for the people and limited the government's ability to act without reason or to abuse its power.

A well known example of a Bill of Rights actively followed and upheld by its people is the one enshrined in the Constitution of the United States. This automatically grants citizens and residents certain civil liberties - including the right to speak or write freely, to assemble when they want, to practise the religion of their choice and to "bear arms". These rights are frequently relied upon in the American courts.

Human rights and civil liberties in the UK

Whilst the UK may not have a written constitution, setting out the civil liberties and rights of its citizens, it has a long common law history of recognising certain freedoms. Indeed, many written constitutions around the world are based on the rights long upheld by the British courts. An example of a very old English right is "Habeas corpus" – which appears to have been in effect in the UK since at least the 14th century and may pre-date the Magna Carta. Under this rule anyone who has been arrested, or deprived of their liberty, may request that they are presented before a

judge so that the legality of their detention can be judicially determined. It has been argued that the spirit of this ancient law has been severely undermined by the introduction of modern anti-terrorist legislation.

The UK Human Rights Act came into force in 2000, giving effect to the European Convention on Human Rights. The rights contained in the Act affect ordinary people in all areas of life – protecting them from breaches of their rights by "public authorities". The Act also made it possible for people to bring a case in a UK court based on a breach of European Convention rights. Prior to the Human Rights Act a British citizen who had their Convention rights breached would have to have gone to the European Court of Human Rights in Strasbourg.

The Human Rights Act requires UK judges to take decisions of the European Court of Human Rights into account when hearing cases. Whenever possible, judges should interpret other UK legislation in a way which is compatible with the European Convention. If it is not possible to interpret existing legislation in a way which is compatible with the European Convention on Human Rights judges may issue a "declaration of incompatibility". This declaration does not affect the validity of a UK Act – which is intended to reflect the principle of Parliamentary sovereignty. An individual may still take his case to the European Court of Human Rights as a last resort.

Civil liberties around the world

In countries all over the world people argue for greater freedoms to be accorded. In America and other Western societies, for example, there have been campaigns to extend the right to marry to all people regardless of their sexuality. In more restrictive countries, some people risk their lives in support of basic civil liberties such as free speech, the right to peaceful protest and freedom of assembly. What constitutes a civil liberty may depend very much on the country that a person calls home.

15 April 2019

UK Human Rights Act is at risk of repeal – here's why it should be protected

An article from The Conversation.

By Stephen Clear

THE CONVERSATION

There have long been attempts to "scrap" the Human Rights Act 1998, which incorporates the European Convention on Human Rights (ECHR) into UK law. But while none have gained traction to date, parliamentarians have recently raised concerns that the government could be wavering in its commitment to the act post-Brexit.

The House of Lords' EU justice sub-committee said in January that it was worried to see the government change the wording of the political declaration it agreed with the EU, which sketches out a non-binding vision for what the UK's relationship with Europe will look like after Brexit.

In its draft form, the declaration said that the future relationship should incorporate the UK's "commitment" to the convention. However, by the time the final version was published in November 2018, that had changed to a commitment to "respect the framework" of the convention.

The committee wrote to the government for clarification and received a response from Edward Argar, the parliamentary under-secretary of state for justice, who stated that the government would not repeal or replace the act while Brexit is ongoing but that "it is right that we wait until the process of leaving the EU concludes before considering the matter further".

Responding publicly, committee chairman Helena Kennedy said that this was a "troubling" reply, noting: "Again and again we are told that the government is committed ... but without a concrete commitment".

Critics of the act say that reforms are needed to "restore" the supremacy of the UK courts, by limiting the interference of the European Court of Human Rights (ECHR) in domestic issues, such as voting rights for prisoners. This has long been a key issue for Conservative governments, which have wanted to ignore Strasbourg rulings. The idea is that the Human Rights Act could be replaced with a "British" bill of rights which would allegedly give the UK more control over the laws it implements.

The most cited criticism is that the act protects terrorists and hate preachers, such as Abu Hamza, who, at a time when he was advocating radical Islam and violence within UK cities, initially could not be deported on grounds that doing so would have contravened his right to freedom from torture.

The successes of human rights laws are less frequently celebrated, however. The act was relied upon by Hillsborough families, and the victims' right to life, in order to secure a second inquiry. Individuals pursuing their freedom to manifest their religion have used it to enforce their right to wear religious symbols at work. Victims of the Stafford hospital scandal used the law to secure an inquiry, which led to major improvements in accountability and public safety. And it has helped those seeking LGBTQ+ equality, as well as British soldiers in their challenge for improved resources.

Dispelling the myths

The problem is that there are several misconceptions fuelling the drive to change the Human Rights Act. First, the ECHR is unrelated to the EU. But mistaken links between the two are causing misplaced animosity towards the convention. The convention and its related institutions were regularly confused as being part of the EU during the referendum debates. Though the UK is due to leave the EU, it is not leaving – and does not necessarily have to leave – the Council of Europe. The council predates the EU, and has a larger membership (47 member states compared to the EU's 28). While the EU is concerned with matters such as the single market and free movement of people, the council addresses issues in relation to human rights and the rule of law.

Another point causing problems is the notion that the UK needs to move towards a supposedly "more British" and "less European" understanding of human rights. History tells us that in the aftermath of World War II the convention was actually partly written by the British. It was advocated by Winston Churchill and co-written by Conservative MP David Maxwell-Fyfe.

Britain was not just a supporter of the convention, but a leader in co-drafting the rules, and ensuring greater enforcement at a supranational level, via the European court. Furthermore, the UK was the very first country to ratify the convention in 1951. The irony is that the Conservative party is now questioning the role of human rights when it was the one that drafted the convention in 1950.

Even if the Humans Right Act was reformed or repealed now, the UK would still be subject to the convention as a signatory. UK citizens would still have access to the protections that the convention has introduced.

If the act is truly under threat of repeal, lessons must be learnt from Brexit. There needs to be an open and honest debate about what the act and convention actually do, and what they have achieved.

If, in repealing the act and introducing a "British bill of rights", the UK leaves the Council of Europe, it could cause a dangerous unravelling of the UK's constitution, and upset the devolution settlement. It could also remove another layer of international protection for the UK's constitutional values. To do so at a time when much uncertainty remains (following the UK leaving the EU) would have far reaching consequences for protecting citizens' rights against the state.

12 February 2019

UK breaches of human rights law

By Louise Smith, barrister

Although the UK has taken well known steps to incorporate internationally recognised human rights law into domestic legislation there are still cases where it is found to have breached human rights. Whilst many cases are resolved within the UK's own legal system, there continue to be cases which go to the European Court of Human Rights (ECHR) for a final decision. We look at some cases where the UK has been found, by the ECHR, to have violated human rights law.

Sexuality of people serving in the UK's armed forces

In 2000 the ECHR found that the UK had violated the human rights of several homosexual soldiers who had been dismissed from the armed forces because of their sexuality. The ECHR ordered the UK to pay substantial damages to the individuals involved. The fact that the soldiers had been questioned about their sexuality, and then dismissed because of it, was held to be a breach of their right to privacy. This case led to the law on the sexuality of those who can serve in the UK's armed forces being changed. The UK is now amongst those countries who allow gay members of the armed forces to be open about their sexuality.

UK widowers' entitlement to benefits

A 2002 human rights case was brought against the UK regarding a widower's entitlement to receive bereavement benefits. Until 2001 a man whose wife had died was not entitled to receive the lump sum and weekly bereavement payments which a woman whose husband had died would receive. A widower who had given up work to care for his children after the death of his wife in 1996, and who was refused the bereavement benefit, took his case to the ECHR. The ECHR held that the widower had been discriminated against on account of his gender and ordered that he be paid £25,000 in damages. By then the law in the UK had already been changed meaning that, today, a bereaved spouse of either gender has equal entitlement to bereavement benefits.

The ban on prisoners voting in the UK

The UK's law preventing prisoners from voting in elections was called into question by a 2005 ECHR case. An ex-prisoner started the case which used human rights law to challenge the UK's ban on prisoners voting. The ECHR held that the ban may constitute a breach of an individual's right to free elections. In 2008, with the UK's law on prisoners voting unchanged, the UN commented that the ban may constitute

a breach of human rights. Although the UK is usually prompt in adapting to ECHR rulings, the ban remains. However, there have been suggestions that the law may be changed to allow some, less serious, categories of prisoner to vote.

Monitoring of private correspondence by the UK government

A 2008 case was brought to the ECHR by several civil rights organisations. This questioned the legitimacy of the UK government's use of phone-tapping and the monitoring of emails between the UK and Ireland from 1990 to 1997. The civil rights groups claimed that some of their correspondence had been monitored by the authorities. The law at that time gave a very wide remit for the UK authorities to monitor

correspondence and the very existence of that law was said by the ECHR to pose a threat to rights and freedoms. The ECHR was concerned that the law was open to abuse and held that the monitoring constituted a breach of the right to private correspondence. The UK government considered the case to be so sensitive in terms of national security, that it would neither confirm nor deny what had actually taken place. However, it did concede that it was reasonable for the ECHR to assume that some of the groups' correspondence had been viewed.

Stop and search under the UK's Terrorism Act

In 2010 the ECHR found that the stop and search procedures used by the UK police pursuant to the Terrorism Act 2000 were illegal because they did not require the police to have grounds for suspicion before using them. The ECHR found that this was open to abuse and constituted a breach of an individual's right to private and family life. Many rules and laws introduced to combat terrorism have been challenged under human rights law. The measures needed to protect the UK against the threat of terrorism are considered to be much greater than those required to combat ordinary crime and there have been concerns from many sectors of society that this has been used as an excuse to take away long-held rights and freedoms.

26 February 2020

There can be no human rights without gender equality

By Bjorn Andersson

- **Recent global gender gains are under threat from growing conservatism.**

- **The universally agreed language of equality is also under attack.**

- **Governments must lead on fighting retrograde forces, supported by civil society.**

'It was the best of times, it was the worst of times.' Charles Dickens' memorable phrase perfectly describes the world of today.

Health and science have advanced as never before. Yet health systems in many countries remain ill-equipped to combat the ongoing COVID-19 outbreak.

We are interconnected more than ever through digital platforms. But the online glue that binds us together virtually has – ironically – sown and amplified real-life divisions, even hatred.

The world has more democracies than ever, but the latest Freedom House report also indicates that democracy and pluralism are under increasing attack.

There are many casualties in this challenging global scenario – truth, compassion, basic decency.

And, not least, human rights and gender equality.

These twin pillars have underpinned landmark global frameworks ever since the founding of the United Nations itself 75 years ago – from the UN Charter of 1945 and the Universal Declaration of Human Rights of 1948, all the way to the Programme of Action that emerged from the 1994 International Conference on Population and Development (ICPD) in Cairo and, a year later, the Platform for Action from the Fourth World Conference on Women in Beijing.

The collective and complementary vision of all of these guide the 2030 Agenda for Sustainable Development and its Sustainable Development Goals, including Gender Equality.

Yes, gains have been made on several fronts globally, including in Asia and the Pacific, in recent decades.

But efforts to advance ICPD, the Beijing Platform and the SDGs are under sustained and concerted attack on multiple fronts in this age of escalating conservatism.

Universally agreed-upon language in UN and other global documents pertaining to sexual and reproductive health and reproductive rights, as envisioned by ICPD, is being targeted by various actors seeking to turn back the clock,

SPOTLIGHT ON
Women in leadership

Women remain under-represented in leadership and management level positions in the public and private sectors. While quotas have been implemented to boost women's participation in politics and corporate boards, parity is far from reality.

Politics

Proportion of women in national parliaments (single or lower house) globally.

2000
13.2%

2017
23.4%

39%
of countries worldwide have used some form of quota system to increase women's representation in politics.

Management

LESS THAN

1/3
of senior and middle-management positions are held by women.*

47%
of world business leaders say they are In favour of gender quotas on corporate boards.

Based on data for 68 countries from 2009 to 2015. Sources: Inter-Parliamentary Union (IPU), www.ipu.org; ILO 2017; International Business Report, 2015.

leading to damaging consequences for women's health in the most resource-challenged countries.

The very concept of gender equality is under threat – and "gender" more than ever serves as a rallying cry for those who would perpetuate patriarchy, sexism and harmful practices against women at multiple levels of government and civil society.

These attacks take aim as well at the rights and well-being of individuals of diverse sexual identities, those living with disabilities and indigenous peoples – groups that have long been marginalized and excluded by society.

How do we counter all of this?

We need governments to demonstrate genuine leadership and be held accountable – with ICPD, Beijing and the SDGs as the yardsticks to be measured and judged by. At the ICPD25 Nairobi Summit last November, 145 countries, including 26 from Asia and the Pacific, made commitments to achieving the Programme of Action, recognising how integral it is to the SDGs – but it's just a start.

We need civil society and communities to be empowered and ever bolder and courageous, to do what is right for women and girls around the world. The #MeToo movement to combat sexual harassment, for example, has gained global traction, but far too many voices remain silenced.

We need to forge a coalition of those who are already champions and those that still need to be convinced by enabling genuine dialogue – using our interconnected, online environment to unite, not divide. We've seen some progress in addressing gender-based violence through wide-ranging coalitions like UNiTE globally and Partners for Prevention in Asia-Pacific. And this year's observance of Beijing25 seeks to bring governments, civil society and the UN together under the umbrella of #GenerationEquality.

We need robust, disaggregated data on women's rights and gender equality to reveal where needs are the greatest, and ensure the inclusion of those furthest behind. The kNOwVAWdata Asia-Pacific initiative, gathering data on the prevalence of violence against women to spur governments to act, is a strong example.

We need to always remember that gains achieved should never be taken for granted. Without human rights, there will simply be no gender equality or women's empowerment – and without gender equality, there can be no realization of human rights.

Twenty-five years after ICPD and the Beijing Platform for Action, let's remain true to the ideals of the remarkable frameworks that were, after all, crafted collectively by countries themselves.

Talk is cheap. Gender equality, women's rights and human rights cannot be values we simply aspire to, but must be regarded as the very foundations that ground humanity itself. These must serve as our collective lodestar, as we navigate this decade of action on the SDGs to a better future for all.

23 March 2020

SPOTLIGHT ON

Sexual & reproductive health

Women face various barriers in exercising their sexual and reproductive health and rights. Migrants and indigenous women, among other marginalized groups, are particularly vulnerable.

ONLY 52%

OF WOMEN MARRIED OR IN A UNION freely make their own **decisions about consensual sexual relations, contraceptive use and health care.**

Percentage of women aged 15-49 years married or in union who make their own informed decisions regarding sexual relations, contraceptive use and health care.
(The number of countries represented in each region in in parenthesis)

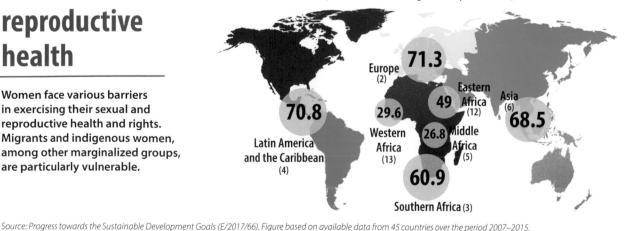

Source: Progress towards the Sustainable Development Goals (E/2017/66). Figure based on available data from 45 countries over the period 2007–2015.

Strengthening children's rights in Scotland

By Daniel McKaveney

The United Nations Convention on the Rights of the Child ('the UNCRC') celebrated its 30th anniversary on 20 November 2019. On the same day, the Scottish Government announced its plans to incorporate the UNCRC into Scots law. This means that the treaty will form part of domestic law in Scotland and its provisions will be enforceable by the courts. This is the result of many years of campaigning by children's rights groups and civil society organisations.

What is the UNCRC?

The UNCRC is the most widely ratified international human rights treaty in history. In total, 196 countries have ratified it, with the USA being the only country in the world that is yet to do so.

It is the most comprehensive statement of children's rights that exists, covering all aspects of a child's life. It includes civil and political rights to economic, social and cultural rights, and even includes rights such as the right to play. Four general principles guide the implementation of the treaty: freedom from discrimination (Article 2); the best interests of the child (Article 3); the right to life, survival and development (Article 6); and the right to be heard (Article 12).

It is also accompanied by 3 additional Optional Protocols. The first and second protect children in armed conflict and from sale and exploitation. The third allows children from Member States who have ratified it to present an official complaint alleging a violation of their rights before the UN Committee on the Rights of the Child, which is the official independent monitoring body of the UNCRC. This protocol was used in September of last year by 16 child climate activists to allege that the failure of their governments to tackle the climate crisis was a violation of their rights.

Like most international treaties, the UNCRC does not dictate exactly how States must implement the treaty at national level. Implementation can, and should, take a variety of forms. This includes both legal and non-legal measures to ensure the realisation of the rights at a domestic level. Article 4 states that "States Parties shall undertake all appropriate legislative, administrative, and other measures for the implementation of the rights recognized in the present Convention". It is therefore up to individual States to decide how best to give effect to the treaty's provisions at national level. There is no single formula that works for every country, and it is dependent on the legal, political and social context in each State, although the UN does consider that incorporation is the first step towards effectively implementing the treaty. This means that the implementation of the obligations and rights under the UNCRC has had varying levels of success across the globe.

The UNCRC in the UK

Although the UK ratified the UNCRC in 1991, it has not incorporated it and so it is therefore non-binding. This is because the UK is a dualist state, meaning domestic legislation is required in order to give effect to an international treaty in domestic law. The UN Committee has recommended that the UK incorporate the UNCRC into its domestic law on several occasions. However, it has not done so and has no plans to do so. The UK does not normally incorporate international treaties into its domestic law. Instead, it has sought to implement the UNCRC through other legal, administrative and non-legal measures. The UK has also ratified the first two additional Optional Protocols, although not the third.

Some of the devolved administrations have taken more progressive steps towards implementing some of the UNCRC's provisions in recent years. For example, in Wales the Rights of Children and Young Persons (Wales) Measure 2011 requires Welsh ministers to have due regard to the UNCRC when making decisions. This is a method of indirect incorporation, as it doesn't incorporate the treaty directly into domestic law, but instead requires decision makers to consider the requirements of the UNCRC when developing policy.

Scotland has also used adopted methods of indirect incorporation. Under the Children and Young People (Scotland) Act 2014, ministers have a duty to keep under consideration whether any steps can be taken in order to better secure the requirements under the UNCRC.

Indirect measures of incorporation such as these can aid in raising awareness of treaties and help further support for more wide-reaching measures in the future.

Scotland's plan

The Scottish Government now plans to incorporate the UNCRC "in full and directly" into Scots law before the current parliamentary session ends next year. A bill will be laid before Parliament this year, and the Government has stated that it will take a "maximalist approach" and incorporate the rights to the maximum extent possible, using the language of the treaty. This means that the treaty will form part of domestic law and will be binding on public authorities and enforceable in the courts. It has said that this is essential in making children's rights real and effective.

In order to inform its plan, the Scottish Government consulted on the incorporation of the treaty from May to August 2019. The consultation looked at three main themes: the different legal mechanisms for incorporating the UNCRC; embedding children's rights in public services; and enabling compatibility and remedies. The vast majority agreed that the treaty should be directly incorporated, and as discussed

this is what the Government intends to do. However, several questions still remain as to what the bill will look like.

The HRA's influence

One of the key issues in the consultation was to what extent the bill should follow the framework of the Human Rights Act 1998, which directly incorporated the European Convention on Human Rights into UK domestic law. The HRA is seen as an effective and "tried and tested" model of directly incorporating an international treaty into domestic law in the UK. It has been successful in ensuring that human rights standards are adhered to by public bodies, and providing redress when they are not.

The majority of respondents to the consultation agreed that the bill should include framework similar to section 6 of the HRA, which prohibits public authorities from acting incompatibly with the ECHR. The bill is likely to draw on other elements of the HRA framework, such as requiring a statement of compatibility to be made when a bill is introduced to the Scottish Parliament, and enabling the courts to declare that legislation is incompatible with the treaty. Ensuring that the treaty's provisions are enforceable in courts and that remedies are available when a violation occurs is also an important aspect of incorporating it.

These aspects of the HRA framework all drew widespread support in the consultation as provisions such as these will ensure that incorporating the treaty results in the effective realisation of rights and is not merely symbolic.

However, many respondents believe that although the HRA framework is a good starting point, the bill that incorporates the UNCRC should go further. As well as a duty to comply

with the UNCRC, a duty on public authorities to have due regard to children's rights has been proposed. This would follow the provisions of the Wales Measure described above. It was argued that this would ensure that a children's rights-based approach was taken when making decisions and developing policy. These two duties would work hand-in-hand and ensure a "proactive and preventative" approach whilst imposing a binding duty on public duties.

Standing

One of the areas where the bill may go further than the HRA framework concerns the rules around who will be able to bring a case to enforce the rights under the UNCRC. Under section 7 of the HRA, individuals can only bring proceedings before a court if they are, or would be, a victim of a violation of the ECHR.

However, many respondents to the consultation considered that having a wider rule in the UNCRC bill would be beneficial. One proposal is the adoption of the "sufficient interest test", which was set out by the Supreme Court in Axa v Lord Advocate [2011] UKSC 46. In this case, the Court held that an individual need not show a personal interest when bringing proceedings if they are acting in the public interest and can demonstrate that the issue directly affects the part of society that they are representing.

There is also widespread support for ensuring that the Scottish Human Rights Commission, the Equality and Human Rights Commission, and the Children and Young People's Commissioner Scotland all have automatic standing.

This wider approach means that individuals would not have to be a victim of a breach of the UNCRC in order to bring proceedings before the courts. Instead, it would allow third parties to raise a challenge before the potential harmful effect of legislation or policy occurred, which is more desirable than waiting for a child to become a victim of a breach.

Comment

The decision to incorporate the UNCRC is a welcome step towards advancing human rights in Scotland. It comes at a time when many are worried about the protection of rights in the UK. The loss of the Charter of Fundamental Rights of the EU due to Brexit; and the Conservative party's pledge to "update" the Human Rights Act highlight these concerns, and we have seen a general regression of human rights standards around the world in recent years.

It is therefore encouraging that Scotland aims to be a leader in the advancement of human rights. As well as incorporating the UNCRC, the Government has established a National Taskforce for Human Rights, following recommendations made by the First Minister's Advisory Group on Human Rights in 2018. This will look at creating a new statutory human rights framework, which may involve incorporating other international human rights treaties, such as the International Covenant on Economic, Social and Cultural Rights, although this will not affect the incorporation of the UNCRC.

Incorporating the UNCRC presents several opportunities. Not only will it provide new legal protections for a group whose rights have often been ignored, it is also an important step towards creating a human rights culture, where rights are a primary consideration in all areas of policy and decision making.

Furthermore, if a wider approach to standing is taken in the bill, this may increase the opportunities to bring public interest litigation before courts. Compared to England, public interest litigation is relatively rare in Scotland, with litigants facing more barriers north of the border. This would be beneficial as public interest plays an important role in democratic society by holding decision-makers to account, developing the law and protecting the rights of vulnerable and minority groups.

However, concerns have been raised that incorporating the UNCRC will only serve to increase the amount of litigation before the courts and will not necessarily result in improving the implementation of children's rights standards. The UNCRC has been criticised more generally for being too broad, with some believing that some of its provisions, specifically those concerning social, economic and cultural rights, are merely aspirational and should not be enforceable. Instead, the priority of States should be on securing civil and political rights. For example, the Scottish Government has been criticised as being hypocritical in its approach to children's rights, as it only raised the age of criminal responsibility from 8 years old to 12. This is despite the UN Committee on the Rights of the Child stating that the absolute minimum age should be 14.

Incorporating an international treaty into domestic law is a complex task. The road to incorporating the UNCRC into Scots law has been long, and questions still remain as to what the bill will look like and whether it will have the desired effect. What is certain is that incorporating the UNCRC is not enough on its own. Further policies, public education and significant funding to support these initiatives are all necessary in order to effect a cultural change and move towards a human rights-based approach. Only then will the rights of every child be real and effective.

24 March 2020

Daniel McKaveney is a graduate of University of Glasgow (Law with Spanish). He is currently working at the Council of Europe in the Human Rights Education for Legal Professionals (HELP) Unit

Human trafficking: scale of the issue

Human trafficking and modern slavery are happening in every corner of the globe.

Given the hidden nature of human trafficking, it is almost impossible to understand the full scope and scale of the issue.

Amongst the most trusted sources for understanding the global situation is the research by the International Labour Organization (ILO).

According to the latest report on forced labour by the ILO:

an estimated 40.3 million victims are trapped in modern-day slavery. Of these:

◆   24.9 million were exploited for labour.

◆   15.4 million were in forced marriage.

There are 5.4 victims of modern slavery for every 1,000 people in the world.

40.3

million victims of human trafficking

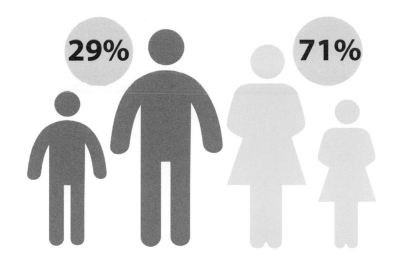

Breakdown

Human trafficking and modern slavery do not discriminate; they affect men and women of all ages.

By gender

71% of trafficking victims around the world are women and girls and 29% are men and boys.

By age

30.2 million victims (75%) are aged 18 or older, with the number of children under the age of 18 estimated at 10.1 million (25%).

◆ 37% victims of trafficking in forced marriage were children.

◆ 21% victims of sexual exploitation were children.

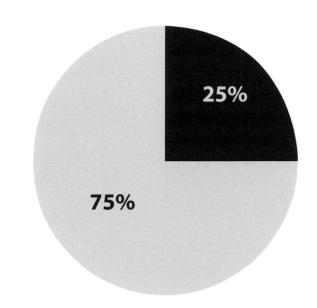

By industry

Forced labour takes place in many different industries.

While every industry is susceptible, those highlighted in the report are broken down as follows:

◆ 16 million (64%) forced labour victims work in domestic work, construction or agriculture.

◆ 4.8 million (19%) persons in forced sexual exploitation.

◆ 4 million (16%) persons in forced labour imposed by state authorities.

Debt bondage

Debt bondage affected half of all victims of forced labour imposed by private actors. Debt bondage is used as a method of control and prevents trafficking victims from escaping.

2018

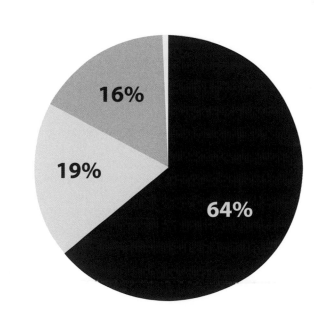

Modern slavery in the UK: March 2020

The hidden nature of modern slavery makes producing an accurate prevalence measure difficult. This article explores the issue and brings together data sources linked to modern slavery from a range of organisations.

Excerpts from the latest release from the Office for National Statistics

Summary

Modern slavery is a serious crime being committed across the UK in which victims are exploited for someone else's gain. It can take many forms including trafficking of people, forced labour and servitude. Victims are often hidden away, may be unable to leave their situation, or may not come forward because of fear or shame.

Because of its hidden nature, producing an accurate measure of prevalence is difficult. Currently, there is no definitive source of data or suitable method available to accurately quantify the number of victims of modern slavery in the UK. Instead, this article brings together a range of available data sources on known victims and cases to provide a better understanding of the extent and nature of this crime.

Greater awareness, increases in reporting and improvements in police recording are likely to have contributed to the increases seen in potential victim numbers since the introduction of the modern slavery Acts across the UK in 2015. For example:

◆ the Modern Slavery Helpline received a 68% increase in calls and submissions in the year ending December 2018, compared with the previous year

◆ there were 5,144 modern slavery offences recorded by the police in England and Wales in the year ending March 2019, an increase of 51% from the previous year

◆ the number of potential victims referred through the UK National Referral Mechanism (NRM) increased by 36% to 6,985 in the year ending December 2018

Collecting legal evidence for modern slavery offences can be difficult, and the cases are among the most challenging and complex to prosecute. For example:

◆ there were 205 suspects of modern slavery flagged cases referred from the police to the Crown Prosecution Service (CPS) for a charging decision in England and Wales in the year ending March 2019

◆ over two-thirds (68%) of modern slavery related CPS prosecutions in England and Wales resulted in a conviction in the year ending March 2019

Modern slavery can affect anyone in society, with victims being exploited in a number of ways. For example:

◆ almost a quarter (23%) of the 6,985 potential victims referred through the NRM in the year ending December 2018 were UK nationals

◆ of the 2,251 potential victims supported by The Salvation Army in England and Wales in the year ending June 2019, 48% had experienced labour exploitation and 39% had experienced sexual exploitation

Defining modern slavery

Modern slavery is a complex crime that covers all forms of slavery, trafficking and exploitation. Trafficking includes transporting, recruiting or harbouring an individual with a view to them being exploited. Modern slavery crimes may involve, or take place alongside, a wide range of abuses and other criminal offences such as grievous bodily harm, assault, rape or child sexual abuse.

Victims of modern slavery can be men, women and children of any age across the world. There is an assumption that victims of modern slavery are often trafficked to the UK from other countries, but residents of the UK are also among the victims that are exploited in the UK and other countries. The crime is often hidden from the authorities and the general public. Victims may struggle to leave their situation because of threats, punishment, violence, coercion and deception, and some may believe that they are not in a situation of exploitation.

The Palermo Protocol, the internationally recognised process for defining human trafficking, includes three aspects:

◆ the action: recruitment, transportation, transfer, harbouring or receipt of persons

◆ the means: threat or use of force or other forms of coercion, of abduction, of fraud, of deception, of the abuse of power or of a position of vulnerability, or of the giving or receiving of payments or benefits to achieve the consent of a person having control over another person

◆ the purpose: the definition of exploitation shall include, at a minimum, the exploitation of the prostitution of others or other forms of sexual exploitation, forced labour or services, slavery or practices similar to slavery, servitude, or the removal of organs

All these aspects must be present for a trafficking crime to have been committed. However, for those under the age of 18 years, only the "action" and "purpose" are required, as children cannot give consent to being exploited regardless of whether they are aware and agree. Victims of modern slavery may be trafficked, but this is not always the case because the "action" may simply involve recruitment.

There are five main types of exploitation that victims of modern slavery may experience:

◆ labour exploitation: victims are forced to work for nothing, low wages or a wage that is kept by their owner; work is involuntary, forced and/or under the threat of a penalty, and the working conditions can be poor

◆ sexual exploitation: victims are exploited through non-consensual abuse or another person's sexuality for the purpose of sexual gratification, financial gain, personal benefit or advantage, or any other non-legitimate purpose

◆ domestic servitude: victims are domestic workers who perform a range of household tasks (for example, cooking and cleaning); some live with their employers and have low pay, if any at all

◆ criminal exploitation: victims are forced to work under the control of criminals in activities such as forced begging, shoplifting, pickpocketing, cannabis cultivation, drug dealing and financial exploitation

◆ organ harvesting: living or deceased victims are recruited, transported or transferred, by threat or force for money, for their organs

The Home Office has published a typology of modern slavery offences, which breaks these exploitation types down further. Because of the nature of the crime, a victim can suffer from multiple exploitation types at the same time or throughout their lifetime. Some data sources included in this article use slightly different definitions of exploitation types.

To combat modern slavery in the UK, legislation was introduced in England and Wales, Northern Ireland, and Scotland:

◆ the Modern Slavery Act 2015 for England and Wales, which received Royal Assent on 26 March 2015

◆ the Human Trafficking and Exploitation (Scotland) Act 2015 for Scotland, which received Royal Assent on 4 November 2015

◆ the Human Trafficking and Exploitation (Criminal Justice and Support for Victims) Act (Northern Ireland) 2015 for Northern Ireland, which received Royal Assent on 13 January 2015

Modern slavery crimes are not new to the UK, and they were punishable against previous offences prior to the introduction of the new Acts in 2015. The new legislation increased the maximum penalties for offences to life imprisonment and introduced further protection and support for victims.

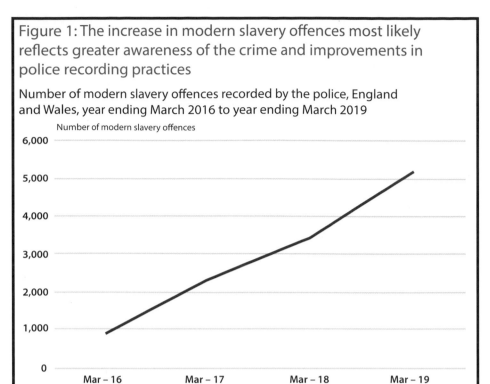

Figure 1: The increase in modern slavery offences most likely reflects greater awareness of the crime and improvements in police recording practices

Number of modern slavery offences recorded by the police, England and Wales, year ending March 2016 to year ending March 2019

Number of modern slavery offences

6,000
5,000
4,000
3,000
2,000
1,000
0

Mar – 16   Mar – 17   Mar – 18   Mar – 19

Police recorded crime

A useful source of data is police recorded crime, which has been badged as a legal and awareness indicator. It demonstrates how modern slavery offences are being reported and recorded following the introduction of the modern slavery Acts. It therefore indicates the police's awareness and visibility of the offences across the UK. Police forces can use these figures to track the number of reported offences geographically, which can inform task forces and investigations.

Data on modern slavery cases that come to the attention of the police provide valuable information. However, they are only a partial picture as many cases remain hidden and not reported or may be recorded as other offences. As police forces adjust to recording against the new modern slavery and trafficking offences, trends are likely to be influenced, meaning it is difficult to make meaningful long-term comparisons.

There are also concerns about the quality and consistency of recording across police forces. In October 2017, data from HM Inspectorate of Constabulary and Fire and Rescue Services's (HMICFRS's) crime data integrity inspection programme established the under-recording of modern slavery offences in England and Wales. To support police forces in improving the identification and understanding of modern slavery, the modern slavery police transformation programme was established. This includes police forces working closely with the National Referral Mechanism (NRM) team to provide clear guidance on the recording of modern slavery offences.

Data from England and Wales, Scotland, and Northern Ireland cannot be combined to calculate the total number of offences in the UK. This is because they use separate offence codes and recording processes. For more information on police recorded crime data, and the legal pathway for modern slavery crimes in the UK.

England and Wales

It is important to note that increases in modern slavery offences are most likely to reflect improvements in recording practices and increases in the general awareness of modern slavery.

Since the year ending March 2016, there has been an increase in the number of modern slavery offences recorded by the police, from 909 to 5,144 offences in the year ending March 2019 (Figure 1). In the year ending March 2019, there was a 51% rise in the number of modern slavery offences being recorded by the police compared with the previous year. Most noticeably, the offence "Require person to perform forced or compulsory labour" doubled in the year ending March 2019 compared with the previous year (from 611 to 1,240 offences).

The most common offences recorded under modern slavery in the year ending March 2019 were "Hold person in slavery or servitude" and "Arrange or facilitate the travel of another person with a view to exploitation". These both contributed to almost three-quarters of all modern slavery offences, which is relatively similar to the previous year (74%). The majority of the remaining offences were recorded as "Require person to perform forced or compulsory labour" (24%).

In the year ending March 2019, where the age and sex of the victim were known in modern slavery offences, the data showed 58% were male and 42% were female.

Scotland

Since the year ending March 2017, there has been an increase in the number of modern slavery offences recorded, from 50 to 179 in the year ending March 2019. Like in England and Wales, these increases are more likely to reflect greater awareness as well as improvements in recording practices, since the introduction of the Human Trafficking and Exploitation (Scotland) Act in Scotland.

Northern Ireland

In the year ending March 2019, there were 38 modern slavery offences recorded. The majority were recorded under "Human trafficking for non-sexual exploitation", which is the same as seen in previous years.

26 March 2020

UK's largest modern slavery gang trafficked more than 400 victims

Vulnerable victims including homeless people and ex-prisoners forced to live in squalor as they earned ringleaders millions.

By Chris Baynes

A human trafficking ring which made £2m by exploiting hundreds of vulnerable victims has been dismantled following the UK's largest modern slavery investigation.

More than 400 people – many of them homeless, ex-prisoners or alcoholics – were forced to work for almost nothing after being lured to the west midlands by a well-organised Polish gang.

The ringleaders told victims they would earn good money in the UK but instead placed them in cramped, rat-infested accommodation and forced them to work on farms, rubbish recycling centres and poultry factories.

They were paid as little as 50p an hour for their labour and in one case a worker was given just coffee and a chicken for redecorating a house.

The victims – aged between 17 and 60 – had to use soup kitchens and food banks to eat, while one man was forced to wash in a canal because he had no other access to water.

'I would say some homeless people here in the UK live better than I lived after I arrived over here,' one victim said.

Meanwhile, the gang's bosses enjoyed a lavish lifestyle off the back of the exploitation, wearing expensive clothes and driving luxury cars including a Bentley.

Eight gang members – who police say were part of two Polish crime families – have been jailed for modern slavery offences and money laundering, it can now be reported, after the second of two trials ended.

A judge said the five men and three women were motivated by greed to exploit their destitute victims and had no 'care or regard for the rights of the individuals affected'.

'The scale of the operation was truly staggering, with millions of pounds netted by the crime group as a result of their callous and systematic exploitation of vulnerable members of the Polish community,' said Mark Paul, head of the Crown Prosecution Service's (CPS) west midlands complex casework unit.

He added: 'Vulnerable men and women were recruited off the streets in Poland with the promise of a better life, only to be cruelly exploited and trapped into a desperate cycle of dependency with nowhere else to go.'

Jurors heard the accounts of 88 victims, but it is believed at least 350 more had passed through the gang's hands and could either not be traced by UK police or were too scared to come forward.

In the most recent trial, a jury at Birmingham Crown Court convicted two of the ringleaders – Ignacy Brzezinski, 52, of Beechwood Road, West Bromwich, and Wojciech Nowakowski, 41, of James Turner Street, Birmingham – of modern slavery offences.

A third, Jan Sadowski, 26, of Dartmouth Street, West Bromwich, admitted his part on the first day of the trial last month.

Sentencing Ignacy to 11 years on Friday, judge Mary Stacey said the 'high functioning alcoholic' had 'direct control' over the trafficking ring and lived 'in the nerve centre of the organisation'.

She added: 'As the head of the family, he set the tone of the operation, and also enjoyed the fruits of the conspiracy, riding round in his Bentley and a fleet of high performance cars at his disposal.'

Ignacy had "abused the compassion of the court" by going on the run following his conviction after being granted bail because he had broken his leg in a fall in court, the judge said.

Nowakowski, who was jailed for six and a half years, was a one-time victim of the ring who had risen to become a 'spy and enforcer' for the gang.

Ms Stacey said: 'He was fully embedded and his role was to keep the conspirators in line.

'Described as a top dog and perhaps a sergeant major, he enjoyed the power over the others.'

Another gang ringleader, Marek Chowanic, was convicted at the end of the first trial in February, along with Brzezinski's cousin Marek Brzezinski, recruitment consultant Julianna Chodakiewicz, the group's matriarch Justyna Parczewska, and Natalia Zmuda.

They were jailed for between four and a half years and 11 years by the judge, who said the victims had endured 'degradation' and a 'demi-life of misery and poverty' at the hands of the gang.

She added: 'Any lingering complacency after the 2007 bicentenary celebrations of the abolition of the English Slave Trade Act was misplaced.

'The hard truth is that the practice continues, here in the UK, often hiding in plain sight.' The Polish gang targeted vulnerable people in their homeland, in some cases waiting at the front gates of prisons to approach people who had just been released.

Victims were housed across at least nine different addresses in West Bromwich, Walsall, Sandwell and Smethwick, crammed up to four to a room, fed out-of-date food, and forced to scavenge for mattresses to sleep on. Some had no working toilets, heating or furniture.

If any complained, gang enforcers would humiliate, threaten or beat them up, while 'house spies' – previously trafficked individuals turned trusted informers – kept an eye on the workers.

Anti-slavery investigators with the charity Hope for Justice and West Midlands Police uncovered shocking brutality against those who stepped out of line.

One man who complained about living conditions and pay had his arm broken and was refused medical care, before being ejected from the accommodation because his injury left him unable to work.

Another was stripped naked in front of other workers, doused in surgical chemical iodine, and told that the gang would remove his kidneys if he did not keep quiet.

The gang seized identity cards, registered victims for national insurance and opened bank accounts in the victims' names using bogus addresses, while their criminal masters also claimed benefits without their knowledge.

The trafficking ring also infiltrated a recruitment agency, meaning work could be directly sourced, without raising suspicions with third parties.

Victims would in some cases be 'frog-marched' to cashpoints to withdraw money and told they owed debts for transport costs, rent and food.

When one worker died of natural causes at an address controlled by the gang, Parczewska ordered that his ID and personal effects be removed from his pockets before paramedics arrived.

Ms Stacey said the conspiracy, which ran from June 2012 until October 2017, was the 'most ambitious, extensive and prolific' modern day slavery network ever uncovered.

The CPS said it believed the gang's convictions marked the largest modern slavery case in Europe to date.

The gang's network collapsed after two victims fled their captors in 2015 and spoke to Hope for Justice.

The charity said 51 of the victims eventually made contact through its painstaking outreach efforts at two drop-in centres.

West Midlands Police then launched an investigation in February 2015.

Opening the second of two trials, Caroline Haughey, prosecuting, said: 'When you are deprived of your freedoms and exploited for your weakness, that is criminal – and it is of such exploitation and degradation that this case concerns – where human beings have become commodities.'

5 July 2019

Children at risk of having their organs harvested flee to UK to escape criminal gangs

By Gabriella Swerling

Children at risk of having their organs harvested are fleeing to the UK to escape criminal gangs, The Telegraph can reveal.

Lungs, kidneys, livers, hearts and corneas are among the most sought-after organs and are sold on the black market around the world for thousands of pounds. Victims are often political prisoners or vulnerable, poor people.

Almost 20 children and adults have been reported to UK authorities in recent years. Last year saw a record number of suspected victims claiming that they had been subjected to one of the most gruesome and harrowing forms of human trafficking and modern slavery.

The disturbing revelation comes as an Independent Tribunal is expected to publish its much-anticipated judgement into forced organ harvesting from prisoners of conscience in China today.

Analysis of National Crime Agency (NCA) data reveals that in 2018, four children and two adults were among those who were flagged to authorities, having claimed that they were under threat of being killed for their organs.

The six referrals to the National Referral Mechanism (NRM) – a scheme designed to support victims of human trafficking and modern slavery – mark the highest since records began.

Between 2012 and 2018, the total number of suspected child and adult victims was 18 and were flagged to the NCA by police, local authorities or charities. However experts warn that this is 'just the tip of the iceberg', with the true number likely to be far higher as although modern slavery is a 'hidden' crime, organ harvesting is particularly traumatic. Its victims are likely to be vulnerable, poor and unable to speak out.

Last year one male adult, one female adult and four young boys ended up in the UK claiming that they were victims of organ harvesting. They hailed from an array of countries including Albania, Vietnam, Iran and Ethiopia. One Polish man ended up in south Yorkshire.

Two of the victims claimed that the location of their suspected exploitation was in the UK. However the NCA confirmed that no cases of organ harvesting occurred in any of the six cases, raising suspicions that for those who claimed that they were exploited in Britain, a deal could have been made by local gangsters to transport the victims elsewhere to harvest their organs.

The NRA is run by the NCA, which publishes data on suspected victims of slavery and trafficking who end up in the UK. It also records the type of exploitation that people of all nationalities claim to have suffered, such as sexual exploitation, forced labour and domestic servitude.

Referrals to the NRM for organ harvesting

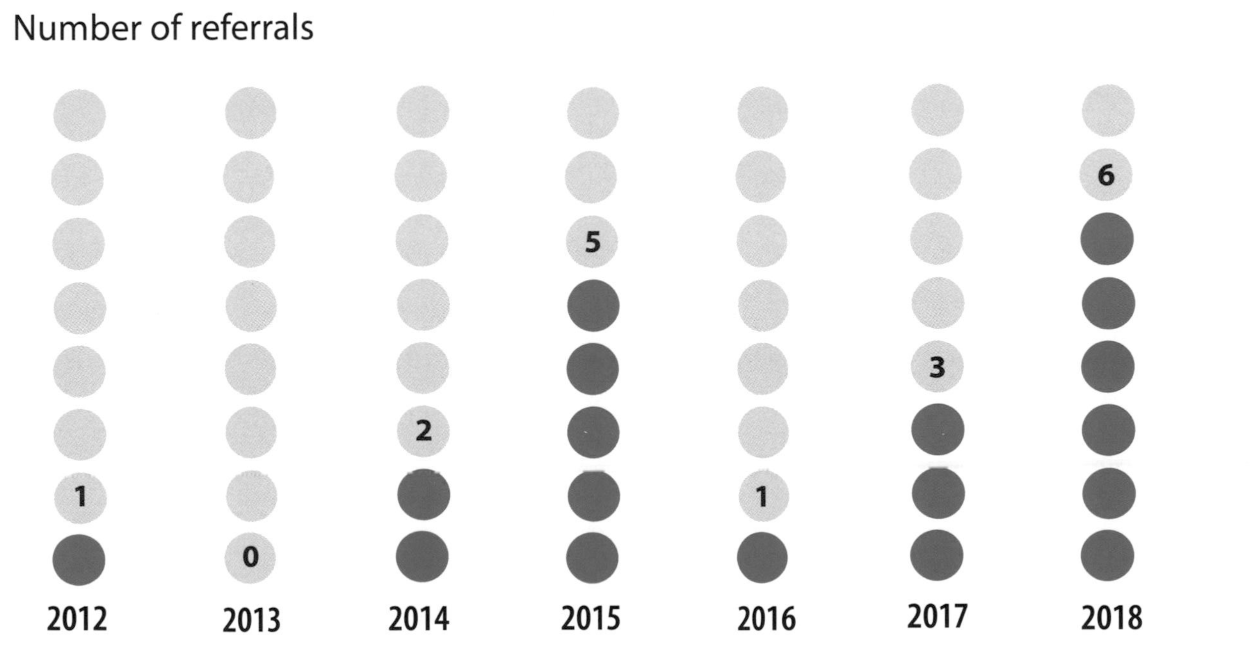

Number of referrals

2012	2013	2014	2015	2016	2017	2018
1	0	2	5	1	3	6

Source: National Referral Mechanism (NRM), National Crime Agency (NCA).

The first case of an individual being trafficked to Britain in order to have their organs harvested was reported in 2012. It is unclear whether the plot was uncovered before the organ removal from the unnamed adult woman took place, but The Salvation Army, which reported the case, said it was the first such case they had seen in Britain.

Mike Emberson, former CEO of the anti-trafficking charity, The Medaille Trust, and an independent expert on modern slavery and human trafficking, said that while it is difficult to extrapolate much detail from such low numbers, cases may be on the increase, or authorities may be better at spotting signs.

However he added: 'What I do suggest, and suggest strongly, is that these figures are very, very low and it is likely, given the scale of the organ trade around the world (of which China is a significant but not sole actor), the recent reports of the scale of OCG [organised crime group] activity in the UK and the various diasporas in the UK who may constitute a significant tranche of the customer base, that we are in the cliched area of 'the tip of the iceberg'.

'It is time for more proactive operations by the NCA and other law enforcement agencies rather than reactive operations instigated after victims are discovered.'

Today an Independent Tribunal, spearheaded by Sir Geoffrey Nice QC, is expected to publish a damning judgement into forced organ harvesting from prisoners of conscience in China.

Sir Geoffrey worked at the International Criminal Tribunal for the Former Yugoslavia and led the prosecution of Slobodan Milosevic. He has compiled a panel of six fellow experts with a variety of backgrounds in international law, medicine, business, international relations and Chinese history.

For decades, China has been accused of forced organ harvesting but has always denied the claims. The country insists that it adheres to international medical standards which require organ donations to be given by consent.

The Tribunal held public hearings in December with 30 fact witnesses, experts and investigators presenting their evidence before the Tribunal in London.

In an interim report, the Tribunal claimed that forced organ harvesting was happening in the country 'beyond reasonable doubt' and that the practice has involved 'a very substantial number of victims'.

It added: 'The Tribunal's members are all certain - unanimously, and sure beyond reasonable doubt - that in China forced organ harvesting from prisoners of conscience has been practised for a substantial period of time involving a very substantial number of victims.'

China was asked to participate in the Tribunal, but has declined to do so.

An NCA spokeswoman said: 'There have been a small number of referrals to the NCA relating to individuals fearing or being threatened with organ harvesting. Traffickers may use the threat of organ harvesting to coerce or control victims, but to date, we have seen no confirmed cases of organ harvesting in the UK.

'The barriers for anyone wishing to harvest organs are substantial. Human traffickers would need corrupt surgeons, medical equipment, operating theatres - which is almost certainly too costly to be a viable criminal enterprise.

'Modern slavery remains a high priority for law enforcement, with over 1400 live operations in the UK.'

16 June 2019

'My mother didn't want me to be cut': female genital mutilation in the UK

Rahma's mother didn't want her daughter to undergo female genital mutilation (FGM), a procedure that involves cutting or removing a girl's labia and clitoris.

By Sian Norris

But when Rahma's aunt discovered the nine-year old hadn't yet been cut, she called an old man to the family home in Somalia. Her aunt told Rahma to lie on the table and open her legs.

'He was so old, I remember he couldn't even see where he was cutting me,' Rahma says. 'He was shaking and I was shaking. My mum was out at work. I was excited because everyone around me had got it done. But it hurt so badly.'

An investigation for The Ferret, funded by the People's Postcode Lottery, has revealed that Rahma is just one of over 22,000 women and girls in the UK identified as having FGM during a healthcare appointment since April 2015. The real number is likely to be much higher, with researchers estimating there could be 137,000 affected women and girls in England and Wales.

Rahma is sitting in the offices of Integrate, a Bristol-based charity committed to ending FGM and empowering young people. Now 18, she has been part of Integrate since she first came to the UK from Somalia and started secondary school. At Rahma's request, her name has been changed to protect her identity.

'I was quite old not to have had FGM. I was in the mosque in Somalia, and all the girls could hear me pee when I went to the toilet,' Rahma says.

'If you've had type three FGM, then you pee really quietly. I came out of the toilets and the girls were staring at me and everyone was talking about how I hadn't had FGM done.

'My auntie couldn't believe my mum hadn't done it – she was like "you're a big girl". She told me she would arrange it.' When Rahma's mother returned home, she found her daughter lying in bed in pain. Rahma says her mum still feels guilty about what happened.

'She says to me that you were vulnerable and I wasn't there for you. But it wasn't her fault. It was my auntie. Mum was against it.'

In the weeks following the FGM, girls like Rahma are told to remain still, with their legs pressed together so the vaginal opening which is stitched together during FGM can close.

'I was moving about because it was painful,' she explains. 'Because my mum didn't want me to get it done, she said I was okay to move around and that it didn't matter if it opened up a bit.

'But when my auntie would visit and see me moving, she'd shout at me. She'd say "why are you doing this, sit down, close your legs together!" So I'd have to, until my mum came home.'

Throughout her adolescence, Rahma has experienced 'painful and heavy periods where it is hard to go out.' Complications around menstruation are a common side effect of FGM.

'Every time my period is painful I cry to my mum and she tells me she's sorry, that this never would have happened if I hadn't got FGM done,' she says.

According to the United Nations (UN), across the world at least 200 million women and girls are living with the impact of FGM. It's defined by the World Health Organisation as comprising 'all procedures involving partial or total removal of the external female genitalia or other injury to the female genital organs for non-medical reasons'.

The UN estimates 68 million more are at risk of undergoing the procedure before 2030. The majority are found across African countries including Somalia, Egypt, and Burkina Faso, as well as in Sri Lanka and Indonesia.

There are three different types of FGM, ranging from type one which is the partial or total removal of the clitoris, to type three which removes the clitoris and labia, and narrows the vaginal opening.

Historically FGM has been justified for religious reasons, although in the UK it is illegal and recognised by the UN as gender-based violence. Some families believe that girls can't be married unless they have undergone FGM and the practice is linked to underage marriage.

Feminist activist Nimco Ali told The Ferret that, no matter what, 'the law says FGM is violence against women and girls, and child abuse.' She is a prominent British campaigner against the practice, who underwent it herself at age seven.

It is not easy to quantify exactly how many girls and women in the UK are like Rahma and living with the impact of female genital mutilation – and how many girls remain at risk. But data from the NHS and academic researchers give a good picture of the scale of the problem.

FGM rates in England

Since April 2015 NHS England has been collecting quarterly data from healthcare providers across the country, including GPs, acute hospital providers and mental health services. This NHS enhanced dataset shows the first time a woman or girl is recorded as having FGM, and all appointments by women and girls recorded as having FGM, including multiple appointments by one person.

Since April 2015 there have been 21,510 newly recorded attendees and 43,005 total attendances. The most recent data, from between April and June 2019, shows 2,905 total attendances by women and girls with FGM, of which 975 were newly recorded.

Many of the attendances involved women and girls in need of medical care related to FGM, but not all. More than three quarters – 78 per cent – of the data collected by NHS England was from women attending midwifery or obstetric appointments.

The majority were in London, where 8,203 women and girls with FGM attended healthcare appointments since April 2015. Over the same period in the north of England there were 4,204, while in the Midlands and the East of England there were 3,908.

Statistics can only be collected when a woman or girl attends a health appointment and is identified as having undergone FGM. This may only happen if she is having a gynaecological procedure, or in need of support for sexual and reproductive health.

Some women simply won't come into contact with healthcare services at all – or have not come into contact with them yet. This is especially true for women with insecure immigration status, who may not feel safe attending a doctor's surgery, let alone disclosing their FGM status.

FGM rates in Wales, Scotland and Northern Ireland

NHS Wales also collects data in order to identify the numbers of women and girls attending healthcare services who have undergone FGM or are in need of medical support as a result of FGM.

In 2018 NHS Wales recorded 271 newly recorded cases of women and girls presenting with FGM – the majority of whom lived in the Cardiff area. This was an increase from 174 the previous year. The total of newly recorded cases from 2016-18 reached 465, with 326 of those cases recorded in Cardiff and Vale University Health Board.

This reflects NHS England's findings that there are more incidences of FGM in busy urban areas than rural regions.

A similar trend was found in Scotland, where the Liberal Democrats used freedom of information requests to reveal 231 cases of women with FGM being treated in Glasgow and Edinburgh. NHS Greater Glasgow and Clyde identified at least 138 women with FGM between 2017-18, and NHS Lothian, which serves Edinburgh, identified FGM on 93 occasions.

In Northern Ireland, data collected by the BBC saw that FGM incidences were again concentrated in the capital: 17 cases were identified in Belfast between 2016-18. Five further cases were recorded in Northern Ireland's Western and Northern health trusts.

Adding these totals to the newly recorded cases in NHS England, public healthcare providers across the UK have identified 22,228 women and girls currently living with the consequences of female genital mutilation. The real figure is likely to be much higher.

The Department of Health and Social Care declined to comment on our findings, referring us to NHS England. 'The FGM Enhanced Dataset is a very powerful dataset in

Female genital mutilation recorded by NHS England

Region	Newly recorded April–June 2019	Newly recorded April 2015–June 2019
London	375	8,203
East of England and Midlands	270	3,908
North of England	250	4,204
South of England	80	1,703
Totals	**975**	**21,510**

Data for April 2015 – June 2015 did not record incidences by region, so the numbers do not total

Source: NHS England

Female genital mutilation in the UK

Nation	FGM cases
England April 15 – June 19	21,510
Wales 2016 – 18	465
Scotland 2017 – 18	231
Northern Ireland 2016 -18	22
Total	22,228

Sources: NHS England, BBC, NHS Greater Glasgow and Clyde, NHS Lothian, NHS Wales

that it is the most comprehensive dataset that we have in understanding the numbers of girls and women with FGM,' said an NHS England spokesperson.

'This has direct implications for the commissioning of services.' The data has already led to a government intervention to ensure better support for women living with the impact of FGM.

In September 2019 eight walk-in FGM clinics opened in England in communities where women are most likely to have been affected. NHS England suggested that this was 'a model of care' for those with lived experience of FGM.

'We do hope that these clinics will be able to create attitudinal change within the community,' added the spokesperson. 'While prevention will hopefully be a product of the service being active in the community, the main focus is to support survivors of FGM with their health and wellbeing needs.'

Breaking the cycle

Some data collected on the prevalence of FGM in the UK is based on the experiences of migrant women who were born elsewhere and then came to the UK as a child or adult – girls like Rahma.

This includes the data gathered and analysed in 2012 by researchers from City University and women's rights organisation Equality Now. They authored a report that sought to estimate the 'numbers of women with female genital mutilation living in England and Wales, the numbers of women with FGM giving birth, and the numbers of girls born to women with FGM'.

They estimated that 137,000 women live with FGM in England and Wales, having collected demographic data about women who had migrated to the UK from countries where it is widely practised, and the girls born to them. The report also derived its estimates by gathering data about the prevalence of FGM 'from reports of household interview surveys in the countries in which it is practised'.

Professor Alison Macfarlane, who co-wrote the City University report, stressed it was important to acknowledge

these estimates were from migrant women. But she added: 'All the available data suggest numbers are now very low among women born in England and Wales.'

This is backed by NHS England data, which shows that far fewer women and girls born in the UK undergo FGM than those born abroad. Between April and June 2019 individual attendances by those born in the UK with FGM was 65, compared to 610 born in the East Africa region where FGM is more prevalent.

The relatively low rate of FGM in girls born in the UK suggests that families from FGM-practising countries are breaking the cycle and getting closer to the UN sustainable development goal to end the practice by 2030.

NHS England, however, was cautious. 'We cannot confirm that the number of girls born in the UK undergoing FGM is low as a result of changing attitudes, due to low reporting rates,' it said.

Macfarlane's 2012 report was followed by an update in 2015 that further identified the risks faced by girls born in the UK. The update found that between 1996-2010, 144,000 girls were born in England and Wales to mothers from FGM-practising countries.

'It was estimated that 60,000 of these girls aged 0-14 were born to mothers with FGM,' the report said. Over half the mothers were from countries where FGM is almost universally practised.

The report urges caution in assuming that all girls born in these families will automatically undergo FGM themselves. 'It is not possible to quantify the prevalence of FGM among girls born in England and Wales to women from FGM-practising countries,' it says.

It explains that even in countries where FGM is common, its prevalence is lower among women with secondary and higher education. 'It is important to recognise the diversity of this group of migrant women and to assess their needs at an individual level,' it adds.

Dr Saffron Karlsen, from Bristol University, agrees. She warned against 'extrapolating data from countries in Africa and Asia and other places where FGM is practised, and applying it to communities living in the UK'.

Karlsen is co-author of a report published in March 2019 called *When Safeguarding Becomes Stigmatising*. The report

Female genital mutilation in Europe

Nation	Estimated population with FGM
Italy	59,716
France	53,000
Germany	47,359
Sweden	38,939
The Netherlands	29,120
Belgium	17,273
Norway	17,058
Spain	15,907
Finland	10,254

Source: The End FGM Europe Network

raises questions about whether safeguarding measures designed to protect girls from FGM have left communities feeling ignored and criminalised, while women's own experiences are dismissed.

'People see the statistics from countries like Somalia and Somaliland,' Karlsen explains, 'which would suggest that 98 per cent of women and girls had FGM. They think therefore 98 per cent of girls born to those women and into those families are at risk.

'But you can't just say 98 per cent of Somali women have FGM, and this many Somali women have moved to this country, and this many Somali women have had children, and so it's 98 per cent of those children that are at risk, regardless of where they live or how their lives might have changed.'

The report authors interviewed focus groups, and found a 'sense of the abuse of a disempowered community pervaded discussions of FGM-safeguarding'.

The report also states that women believed medical staff collecting information for the NHS enhanced dataset prioritised extracting information required for government statistics. They felt the need to gather data ignored women's 'health needs'.

At worst, it failed to consider 'their trauma in connection with their past experiences of FGM' or how their experiences of safeguarding might exacerbate that, the report says.

Karlsen heard from women in Bristol's Somali community who were not supportive of FGM. 'They felt very strongly that their children should be protected from FGM and were very keen to be involved in working with different authorities and groups towards ending FGM,' she says.

'They didn't see FGM as an issue in their culture anymore. They said their culture had changed, and FGM was now in the past.'

Rahma's own family has broken the cycle of FGM. As well as her activism and her mother's opposition to the practice, she said her brothers and father were 'very against' it. She believes that most people in the Somali community in Bristol also oppose it, but she adds: 'There's a lot of work to do.'

Listening to women

Both Rahma and Karlsen agree that women and girls must be listened to if FGM is to be ended. This means focusing on the experiences of victims and survivors.

They point out that the women and girls affected can provide a vital insight into what safeguarding should look like, the challenges they face, and how public health policy can respond to their needs.

Rahma knows all too well how important it is for women and girls to have spaces where they can raise their voices. Being involved with Integrate has helped her develop her confidence and speak out about her own experiences of FGM.

'I told my friends I was a survivor and they couldn't believe it,' she says. 'They told me they thought girls who had had it done were quiet and shy. But you need to speak about it. Integrate has helped me to come out and feel good about myself and talk about what happened.'

Integrate's director, Lisa Zimmermann, agrees the momentum to end FGM has to be centred on the experiences and voices of young survivors, including the "amazing young activists" she works with.

'When we first started in 2007 no one was talking about FGM, Zimmermann says. 'Today so much has changed, and it's survivors who are leading the work. That's wonderful to see.'

Now Rahma hopes to work in healthcare so she can help other women who have undergone female genital mutilation. But most of all she wants to see a future where the practice has ceased for good.

'I really, really hope that no one has to go through that kind of pain,' she says. 'Hopefully we can all come together and fight this as a whole.'

She takes a deep breath. 'And end it.'

21 November 2019

Child marriage

More than 250 million women alive today were married before their 15th birthday, many against their will. Child marriage robs them of their childhoods, education, health and freedom, and can leave girls vulnerable to abuse for the rest of their lives.[1]

Girls living in the poorest, rural areas of sub-Saharan Africa and South Asia are the most vulnerable. As populations continue to grow, hundreds of millions of girls remain at risk.

Local ActionAid workers are working to end child marriage in their communities – bringing perpetrators to justice, educating communities on the negative effects of child marriage, and empowering girls to have a voice and say no.

ActionAid also campaigns at a regional, national and international level to end forced marriage.

What is the difference between child marriage, forced marriage and arranged marriage?

Child marriage is any formal marriage or informal union where one or both people are under 18 years old.

A forced marriage is where one or both people do not consent to the marriage and pressure or abuse is used. Pressure can include threats, physical or sexual violence, and financial pressure. This is different to an arranged marriage, where both people have consented to the union but feel free to refuse if they want to. All child marriages are forced, because a child cannot provide informed consent, and are therefore a violation of children's rights.

Child marriage also affects boys, but to a lesser degree than girls. In the Central African Republic, the country where boys are most likely to be married in childhood, the levels of child marriage among girls are still more than twice those seen among boys.[2]

Where does child marriage happen?

Child brides can be found in every region in the world, from the Middle East to Latin America, South Asia to Europe. It is a global problem.

In the UK, the Home Office's Forced Marriage Unit supported over 1,400 suspected cases of forced child marriage in 2016.[3]

But rates of child marriage are most prevalent in sub-Saharan Africa – in countries such as Niger (76%) and Central African Republic (68%), and in South Asia – in countries such as Bangladesh (52%), and India (47%).[4]

In many communities across these regions, girls are being violently abducted before being forced to marry their captors, usually many years older than them.

What are the causes of child marriage?

Despite laws against child marriage in most countries, various exceptions to the minimum age undermine these laws and make them difficult to enforce. Exceptions include parental consent, authorisation of the court, or local customary or religious laws.

The reasons for child marriage differ from country to country, but in sub-Saharan Africa and South Asia – where the practice is most widespread – the key drivers are gender inequality, and poverty.

Gender inequality

Deep-rooted patriarchal beliefs, the low value placed on girls, and the desire to control women, especially girls' sexuality, underlie child marriage.

Social expectations and norms around the world expect girls to become wives and mothers, and in poorer communities with limited opportunities for education and work it may seem like the alternatives are limited. Even if opportunities are available, social norms that value boys over girls and support rigid gender roles means parents might not think it worthwhile investing in their daughter's education.

Child marriage is also closely linked to female genital mutilation (FGM) – the partial or full cutting of a girl's clitoris and labia for non-medical reasons – which is considered essential for marriage in many communities, particularly in sub-Saharan Africa.

The social stigma of not following tradition ensures the practice continues.

Child marriage facts

250m: Worldwide, more than 250 million women alive today were married before their 15th birthday, many against their will.[5]

17%: 17% of the world's child brides live in Africa – that's 125 million.[6]

15m: 15 million girls are forced to marry each year – that's 28 girls a minute.[7]

Pauline's story

Pauline was married in exchange for cows

'I did not choose my husband,' says 15-year-old Pauline from West Pokot, Kenya. 'I don't like him, but I have to because he is my husband.'

Forced to leave school because her parents couldn't pay anymore, Pauline had FGM, aged 10, and was married off shortly afterwards.

'My parents wanted me to get married off so as to get some cows,' she explains. 'I could not have avoided it. I did not know that the cut [FGM] meant that I would then be forced to be married. I knew nothing about marriage or pregnancy.'

Pauline has a baby girl, Faith, with her husband, and is pregnant with their second child. She is now part of an ActionAid-supported women's group working to advocate against FGM and child marriage.

Poverty

Poverty is the other major driver. In Africa, for example, girls from the poorest households are twice as likely to marry before age 18, as girls from the richest households. Similarly, girls in rural areas are twice as likely to become child brides as girls from urban areas.[8]

For poor families with many children, marrying their daughter off early can mean one less mouth to feed. In addition, there is also a financial aspect due to dowry and bride price traditions.

Dowry and bride price

A dowry, most common in South Asia, is when the bride's family pays the groom's family in money, goods or property. Usually, the younger the age of the girl bride, the lower the dowry, giving parents an incentive to marry their daughters young.

Bride price, most common in sub-Saharan Africa, is the other way round – the groom's family pays the bride's family. The price is often intended to reflect the value of the bride, perpetuating the concept of girls as a commodity and as men's property.

Disagreements over dowries and bride price sometimes cause family disputes that can result in violence.

What are the effects of child marriage?

Child marriage is an act of violence and a violation of girls' rights. It denies them their childhood, the chance to go to school, to be independent and to choose their own future.

Extremely vulnerable to violence

Girls who marry as children are often married to older men, which intensifies power imbalances in the relationship. Subordinate to their husbands and families, domestic violence by an intimate partner is more prevalent and more severe amongst girls who marry as children, than amongst women who provide informed consent to marry.[9]

For many girls child marriage subjects them to rape and abuse for the rest of their lives. Isolated from friends and family they have limited means to get support or share what they are going through.

Health and lives at risk

With limited education and decision-making power, girls are not in a position to influence decisions over safe sex and family planning, which puts them at high risk of sexually transmitted diseases including HIV, and of giving birth before their bodies are ready.

Girls are physically unprepared for childbirth, because of the restrictions in movement they face as a girl-child in their community, lack of access to sexual and reproductive health and rights information, as well as not being biologically mature enough to give birth.

Early childbearing puts girls' lives at risk, and increases the chance of stillbirth, infant mortality, and disabling complications for the mother such as obstetric fistula.

Globally, 16 million girls aged between 15 and 19, and 1 million girls under the age of 15, give birth each year.[10] 70,000 girls die during pregnancy and childbirth. This makes complications during pregnancy and childbirth the second highest cause of death for girls aged 15-19 worldwide.[11]

For girls who have also had female genital mutilation (FGM), sex and giving birth can be excruciatingly painful, and they are at far higher risk of complications from childbirth.

Education cut short

When girls' education is cut short, girls lose the chance to learn the knowledge and skills they need to secure a good job and provide for themselves and their families. Girls who have little or no education are up to six times more likely to be married as children than girls who have secondary schooling.[12]

They also lose the opportunity to be empowered, make friends, and develop social networks and confidence that will help them stand up for their own interests.

As a result, millions of girls continue to be held back and remain living in poverty.

How ActionAid is working to stop child marriage

ActionAid works to end child marriage in 17 countries across South Asia and sub-Saharan Africa. Our local staff tackle it on many fronts – from bringing perpetrators to justice, to changing minds and behaviours in local communities, to campaigning at a regional, national and international level to influence policies and legislation to end violence against girls.

17: ActionAid works to end child marriage in 17 countries across South Asia and sub-Saharan Africa

322,000: women helped to challenge violence against women and girls and harmful traditional practices like FGM (in 2016 alone)

1,080: community-led projects to support women and girls to challenge harmful traditional practices including FGM (in 2016 alone)

ActionAid trains and supports local networks of women and men to reach out to their neighbours, families, officials and village leaders to highlight the negative effects of early child marriage and pregnancy, and how keeping girls in school can benefit the whole community.

Educated girls are better equipped to contribute to their own well-being and that of their future families, and contribute to reducing poverty in their communities and countries as a whole.

The community-led anti-violence teams (COMBAT) confront the perpetrators of child marriage directly, either face to face or through formal letters, and work to ensure girls at risk are returned to their families. If captors do not co-operate, the teams work with the authorities to bring them to justice.

ActionAid trains female teachers to run girls' clubs in schools and communities, to empower girls to understand and live out their rights, including saying no to child marriage. The women are role models to the girls, showing them that finishing their education is possible.

Bespoke solutions for different communities

Because the way that children are married off varies from country to country, it is vital to work with communities to find specific solutions to protect girls becoming child brides.

For example, in the Upper West Region of Ghana, many teenage girls are being violently abducted on their way to school to be forced into child marriage. Local ActionAid staff reports that more than 50 girls a year are being taken.

Girls are most at risk during the rainy season, when they must walk through fields of long grass to get to school. Men are often waiting to capture them, and take them by motorbike to faraway villages when they least expect it.

One initiative ActionAid is using to prevent this happening, with great success, is giving bicycles to girls at risk of forced marriage. The bikes have two functions: personal safety – the bikes cut down the girls' long and dangerous route to school, and the ActionAid stamp deters abductors from harming them, and secondly – with a faster journey, more girls are staying in school, and girls in education are less likely to be married young.

Globally, the practice of child marriage is slowly declining, but as populations grow, hundreds of millions of girls will continue to be at risk. Unless we speed up progress to end child marriage, the global number of child brides will remain the same by 2050 (at 700 million).

2018

Footnotes

1   UNICEF (2015), 'A profile of child marriage in Africa'
2   UNICEF (2015), 'A profile of child marriage in Africa'
3   UK Home Office (2017), 'Forced Marriage Unit Statistics 2016'
4   UNICEF (2016), 'State of the World's Children'
5   World Health Organisation (2016), 'Violence against women, intimate partner and sexual violence against women'
6   UNICEF (2015): 'A profile of child marriage in Africa'
7   The Lancet (2015), 'Prevention of violence against women and girls: what does the evidence say?'
8   UNICEF (2015): 'A profile of child marriage in Africa'
9   Spencer, D. (2015), 'To protect her honour: Child marriage in emergencies – the fatal confusion between protecting girls and sexual violence'
10 World Health Organisation (2014), 'Adolescent pregnancy'
11 World Health Organisation (2014), 'Adolescent pregnancy'
12 UNICEF (2015), 'A profile of child marriage in Africa'

5 human rights issues that defined 2019

An article from The Conversation.

THE CONVERSATION

By Elaine Pearson, Adjunct Lecturer in Law, UNSW and Louise Chappell, Director of the Australian Human Rights Institute; Professor of Law, UNSW

As we approach the last days of the decade, it's important to reflect on the fight for human rights, the setbacks and successes over the past year in Australia and around the world.

Our list isn't ranked, and far from exhaustive – we acknowledge it doesn't include many human rights struggles worthy of greater attention. But, in flagging some of the issues needing urgent attention, we hope to gather support for the broader movement that strives to achieve justice and secure dignity for more people.

China holding one million Muslims in 'political education camps'

China is arbitrarily detaining an estimated one million Muslims in Xinjiang, in what the authorities call "political education camps". Millions more are subjected to intrusive mass surveillance.

Leaked internal Chinese Communist Party documents described in chilling detail just how the Chinese authorities keep the Uighurs locked up.

The size of your beard, where you travel and whether you use the back door of the house are all potentially indicators of 'terrorism' that can send you to the camps with no legal process at all.

The leaked documents are consistent with previous reporting on Xinjiang, but reveal the campaign originated from President Xi Jinping himself. They dispel the Chinese government's claims these camps are merely 'vocational training centres'.

More than two dozen countries joined two United Nations statements in Geneva and New York urging China to end this arbitrary detention of Muslims.

In response, China organised several dozen countries, including notorious rights abusers such as Russia, Egypt, and the Democratic Republic of Congo, to join statements commending China for its counter-terrorism efforts.

Faced with the growing body of evidence of large-scale human rights violations backed by China's leadership, the question is whether the rest of the world will hold the Chinese government to account in 2020.

Some women in Saudi Arabia can travel freely

Following unprecedented global attention on Saudi Arabia's discriminatory male guardianship system, which restricts women's rights to travel (among other things), Saudi authorities undertook reform.

At last, Saudi women over 21 years old have the right to travel abroad freely and obtain passports without permission from their male guardian. But this is a shallow victory for Saudi women, who still face myriad rights abuses at home.

Activists remain locked up for peaceful acts of free expression, some alleging they have been tortured.

The Saudi government also hasn't taken meaningful steps to provide accountability for the murder of journalist Jamal Khashoggi, or for their alleged war crimes in Yemen.

Australia's performance on the UN Human Rights Council

After initially taking a low-key approach to its membership in the UN Human Rights Council, Australia stepped up in its second year. This was to ensure the council renewed the mandate of the special rapporteur on Eritrea, where human rights continue to deteriorate.

In September, Australia led a joint statement bringing attention to human rights violations by Saudi Arabia, and the government joined two UN statements on Xinjiang.

In 2020, the final year of Australia's membership term, the government should keep up the pressure on Saudi Arabia and China by pressing for independent international inquiries into longstanding abuses.

Aged care: a shocking tale of neglect

"A shocking tale of neglect" was the headline of the Royal Commission's interim report into the Australian aged care system.

Tabled in the federal parliament in October, the report revealed more than 270,000 cases of substandard care in Australian nursing homes in the past five years. It argued for a major overhaul to transform the way Australia supports people as they grow older.

One of the issues the commission heard testimony on was the routine use of drugs to control the behaviour of older people with dementia, without a medical purpose.

This practice is known as chemical restraint, and the drugs have devastating effects. They increase the risks of falls or strokes, and can render previously energetic people lethargic and, in some cases, unable to speak.

A Human Rights Watch report detailed the practice in 35 aged care facilities in Australia, and its impact on residents and their families.

It called for the government to prohibit chemical restraint and ensure adequate staffing with appropriate training to support people with dementia.

Water rights under threat in Australia

Australians saw the haunting image of dead and dying fish in Australia's most important river system, the Murray Darling.

Scientists concluded exceptional climatic conditions influence this "serious ecological shock" in a river system that now has very little water to serve the needs of people, agriculture and a fragile environment.

The right to clean drinking water, recognised under international human rights law, is already under threat for people in some rural and remote communities across New South Wales and Queensland. And it will become more relevant as droughts exacerbated by climate change continue to bite Australian cities and towns.

In the Northern Territory community of Laramba, 250 kilometres northwest of Alice Springs, the level of uranium in the drinking water is more than double the level recommended in the Australian Drinking Water Guidelines. It prompted legal action against the territory's government.

What's more, for the first time since records were kept, on November 11 no rain was recorded on continental Australia.

Youth-led climate justice movements

One of this year's most refreshing developments was the youth-led action on climate change. It brought together environment and human rights concerns, inspiring an estimated 300,000 Australians to join a global strike in September.

For some, it was a way to demonstrate outrage at the federal government's weak position and lack of action to address climate change.

For others, the enormous fires in the precious Amazon forest, fuelled by violence and impunity, was compelling.

And, of course, many were moved to strike because of the brave and passionate voices of Greta Thunberg and other children who are demanding action for the sake of future generations.

We hear them loud and clear – and call on Australia's leaders to listen and act.

10 December 2019

Facial recognition technology 'violates human rights and must end', landmark court case hears

First legal challenge against UK police trials of facial recognition to set precedent.

By Lizzie Dearden, Home Affairs Correspondent

Police are breaking human rights law with the use of controversial facial recognition software, a landmark court case has heard.

Ed Bridges is bringing the first legal challenge on the technology, which has been trialled by forces in different parts of the UK.

He believes he was scanned by cameras used by South Wales Police at a peaceful anti-arms trade protest in 2018 and while doing his Christmas shopping in Cardiff months before.

Mr Bridges said police started using facial recognition 'without warning or consultation'.

He added: 'It's hard to see how the police could possibly justify such a disproportionate use of such an intrusive surveillance tool like this. We hope that the court will agree with us that unlawful use of facial recognition must end, and our rights must be respected.'

Lawyers accused the force of violating Mr Bridges' privacy and data protection rights by processing an image taken of him in public.

Dan Squires QC told the Administrative Court in Cardiff that automatic facial recognition (AFR) allowed police to 'monitor people's activity in public in a way they have never been able to do before' without having to gain consent.

He said: 'The reason AFR represents such a step change is you are able to capture almost instantaneously the biometric data of thousands of people. It has profound consequences for privacy and data protection rights, and the legal framework which currently applies to the use of AFR by the police does not ensure those rights are sufficiently protected.'

Mr Bridges had a reasonable expectation that his face would not be scanned in a public space and processed without his consent while he was not suspected of wrongdoing, Mr Squires said.

The lawyer argued that police had violated article eight of the Human Rights Act - respect for privacy - as well as the Data Protection Act.

Mr Squires said there was no statutory power which permitted South Wales Police to perform large-scale processing of people's data without their consent, and called for a code of conduct to be drawn up.

Facial recognition scans faces from live camera footage and compares results with a 'watch list' of images from a police

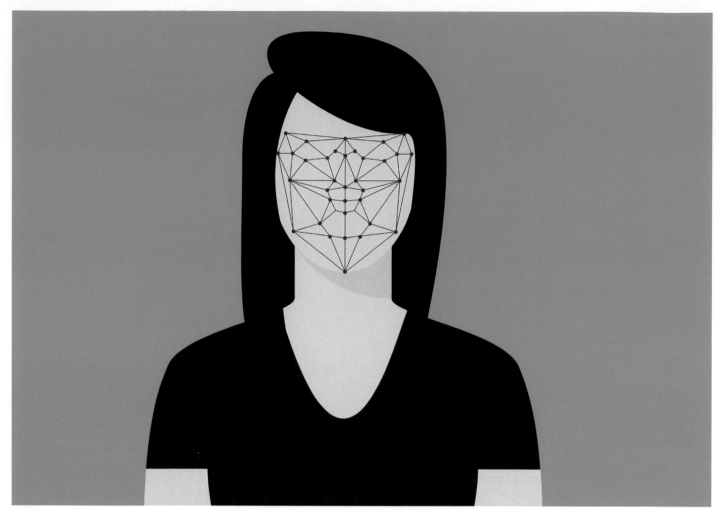

database, which can use varying parameters set to include suspects, missing people and persons of interest.

The court heard that South Wales Police had deployed facial recognition at least 40 times since it began trialling it May 2017, with no end date set.

The force argues that use of AFR does not infringe the privacy or data protection rights because it is used in the same way as photographing a person's activities in public.

It said it does not permanently retain the data of people who are not confirmed as a match to its watchlist, but does keep CCTV images from the scanning process for up to 31 days.

Mr Bridges raised almost £6,000 for the judicial review, writing on a fundraising website that the public 'had not be consulted' on facial recognition.

'The police are supposed to protect us and make us feel safe – but I think the technology is intimidating and intrusive,' he added. 'There's not even any guidance on how to deploy it, and no independent oversight to make sure its use is appropriate and our rights are protected.'

Ed Bridges brought a legal challenge against South Wales Police over its use of facial recognition technology.

He is being supported by the Liberty human rights charity, which said facial recognition 'makes a mockery of our right to privacy'.

Lawyer Megan Gouldin said: 'It is discriminatory and takes us another step towards being routinely monitored wherever we go, fundamentally altering our relationship with state powers and changing public spaces. It belongs to a police state and has no place on our streets.'

Studies have shown some facial recognition software disproportionately misidentifies women and ethnic minorities, while a man was fined after covering his face in London.

South Wales Police did not seek to block the challenge and its chief constable indicated that he would welcome guidance on complex legal and ethical issues. Jeremy Johnson QC will set out the force's response to the case.

London's Metropolitan Police is facing a separate legal challenge over its own facial recognition trial, which has seen members of the public misidentified as criminals in 96 per cent of scans.

The trials have so far cost more than £222,000 in the capital alone and are subject to a separate probe by the Information Commissioner.

Additional reporting by Press Association

21 May 2019

Ten ways that Saudi Arabia violates human rights

In February 2015, the Saudi Arabian authorities publicly flogged blogger Raif Badawi, sentenced to 1,000 lashes and 10 years in prison for 'insulting Islam' and founding an online forum for political debate.

Due to be flogged 50 times every week, Raif's lashes have so far been postponed on a weekly basis. For the first couple of weeks in January, the authorities cited medical advice given by doctors who examined Raif, who had found his wounds 'hadn't healed enough' for him to be flogged again 'safely'. Latterly, the Saudi Arabian authorities have refrained from flogging Raif, without giving a reason. He continues to be told on a weekly basis whether his 950 lashes will begin again that week.

Raif has made headlines around the world. But his case is just the tip of the iceberg for the Gulf Kingdom's appalling human rights record.

Here are ten ways Saudi Arabia is violating its citizens' human rights:

1. Torture is used as a punishment

Courts in Saudi Arabia continue to sentence people to be punished by torture for many offences, often following unfair trials. Corporal punishment like flogging, for example, is a cruel, inhuman and degrading punishment that has no place in the justice system.

Besides Raif, in the past two years the human rights defenders Mikhlif bin Daham al-Shammari and Omar al-Sa'id were sentenced to 200 and 300 lashes respectively, and Filipino domestic worker Ruth Cosrojas was sentenced to 300.

There are other forms of torture issued as punishment: Saudi authorities have carried out amputations, including 'cross amputations' (where the opposite hand and foot are removed) on people found guilty of robbery.

2. Executions are on the increase

Saudi Arabia is among the world's top executioners, with dozens of people being executed by the state every year, many of them in public beheadings.

So far this year Saudi Arabia has executed 40 people – almost four times as many as the same period last year.

3. No free speech

Besides Raif Badawi, dozens more outspoken activists remain behind bars, simply for exercising their rights to freedom of expression, association and assembly.

In the last two years, all of Saudi Arabia's prominent and independent human rights defenders have been imprisoned, threatened into silence, or fled the country. The authorities have targeted the small but vocal community of human rights defenders, including by using anti-terrorism laws to suppress their peaceful actions to expose and address human rights violations.

4. No protests

Going to a public gathering, including a demonstration, is a criminal act, under an order issued by the Interior Ministry in 2011. Those who defy the ban face arrest, prosecution and imprisonment on charges such as 'inciting people against the authorities'.

5. Women are widely discriminated against

Women and girls remain subject to discrimination in law and practice, with laws that ensure they are subordinate citizens to men - particularly in relation to family matters such as marriage, divorce, child custody and inheritance.

Women who supported a campaign against a ban on women drivers face the threat of arrest and other harassment and intimidation.

6. Torture in police custody is common

Former detainees, trial defendants and others have told us that the security forces frequently use torture in detention, and that those responsible are never brought to justice.

7. You can be detained and arrested with no good reason

Scores of people have been arrested and detained in pre-trial detention for six months or more, which breaches the Kingdom's own criminal codes. Detainees are frequently held incommunicado during their interrogation and denied access to their lawyers. Some human rights activists have been detained without charge or trial for more than two years.

8. Religious discrimination is rife

Members of the Kingdom's Shi'a minority, most of whom live in the oil-rich Eastern Province, continue to face entrenched discrimination that limits their access to government services and employment. Shi'a activists have received death sentences or long prison terms for their alleged participation in protests in 2011 and 2012.

9. Migrant workers have been deported en masse

According to the Interior Ministry, a crackdown on irregular foreign migrant workers in November 2013 led to the deportation of more than 370,000 people. Some 18,000 were still being detained last March. Thousands of people were summarily returned to Somalia, Yemen or other states where they could face human rights abuses on return.

10. Human rights organisations banned

The Saudi Arabian authorities continue to deny access to independent human rights organisations like Amnesty International, and they have been known to take punitive action, including through the courts, against activists and family members of victims who contact us.

12 January 2018

Saudi Arabia executed record number of people in 2019, human rights group says

Increase in executions follows crown prince's 2018 pledge to 'minimise' use of death penalty.

By Conrad Duncan

Saudi Arabia executed 184 people in 2019, the highest number of killings since records began six years ago, according to human rights campaigners.

Research by Reprieve, an organisation which tracks human rights abuses, showed a record number of executions compiled from reports by the official Saudi Press Agency, including one example where 37 people were executed in a single day.

Press reports showed 90 of those killed were foreign nationals, while 88 were Saudi nationals and 6 were of unknown nationality.

The figures also showed that executions have more than doubled in Saudi Arabia since 2014, when 88 people were killed, with 2019 being comfortably the worst year for killings.

In comparison, 149 people were executed in 2018 and 146 people were killed in 2017, according to Reprieve.

The research came after Saudi Crown Prince Mohammed bin Salman said his government was trying to 'minimise' the use of capital punishment in the country in 2018.

'These latest execution figures expose the gap between the reformist rhetoric and bloody reality of Mohammed bin Salman's Saudi Arabia,' Maya Foa, the director of Reprieve, told The Independent.

'As the Crown Prince travels the world meeting heads of state, his regime has been executing young men arrested as children for the 'crime' of standing up for democracy.'

Ms Foa also criticised the upcoming G20 summit in the capital of Riyadh which is set to take place in November this year.

'2020 must be the year that the Kingdom's partners stop falling for the Saudi charm offensive and insist on an end to these egregious human rights abuses and violations of international law,' she added.

The event has already drawn criticism from the human rights group Amnesty International, who have refused to attend G20 meetings in preparation for the annual summit.'

'We cannot participate in a process which is being abused by a state which censors all free speech, criminalises activism for women's and minority rights, as well as homosexuality, and tortures and executes critics,' the group said in a statement.

Saudi Arabia has sought to improve its international reputation in recent years with 'expensive PR campaigns' and high-profile sporting events, Amnesty added.

In a 2018 interview for Time magazine, the Saudi crown prince claimed his government was looking into reducing the number of executions and said he believe it would take about one year to introduce reforms.

However, the following year saw no reductions in the number of executions.

In April, the country carried out one of the largest mass executions in its history, in which 37 people were sentenced to death.

CNN reported that many of the men who were condemned to death had been sentenced on the basis of confessions which were obtained by coercion and torture.

14 January 2020

In a dangerous world, human rights activists have been winning all year

With inequality, injustice and hate speech seemingly ever more prevalent across the globe, you'd be forgiven for thinking 2019 has been a bad year for human rights. Yet, we have also seen some significant wins. Activists the world over have been galvanised to stand up and fight for our human rights – and thanks to their relentless campaigning we achieved some striking leaps forward. Here are some highlights…

January

Legal abortion services were finally available to women in Ireland, following an historic referendum in May 2018 that marked a huge victory for women's rights. It was the result of years of dedicated work by activists, including Amnesty International, to encourage a powerful conversation that helped catalyse the abortion debate in Ireland. This ultimately led to greater protection for those people who need an abortion there, and paved the way for the same inspiring progress in Northern Ireland later in the year.

As a tribute to Julián Carrillo, an environmental rights defender killed in October 2018, we launched Caught between bullets and neglect, a digest on Mexico's failure to protect environmental human rights defenders. Just a few hours after the launch, two suspects in Julián's murder were arrested, showing the immediate impact Amnesty's work can have on justice.

The Angolan Parliament approved a revision of the Criminal Code to remove a provision widely interpreted as criminalizing same-sex relationships. They even took a step further, by criminalizing discrimination against people based on sexual orientation – the first country in 2019 to make this move, and a hearteningly radical move for an African nation.

February

After spending 76 days in detention in Thailand, refugee footballer Hakeem al-Araibi was able to return to his home in Melbourne on 12 February. The Bahrain-born footballer had been detained upon arrival in Bangkok on 27 November 2018, due to an erroneous Interpol red notice, and faced the threat of extradition to Bahrain. A campaign launched by Amnesty and other groups to free the footballer, who is a peaceful and outspoken critic of the Bahraini authorities, grew into the #SaveHakeem movement. The campaign spanned three continents, engaging footballers, Olympians and celebrities, and drawing the support of more than 165,000 people.

Following international attention and campaigning by Amnesty, Saudi authorities overturned a call by the Public Prosecution to execute Saudi woman activist Israa al-Ghomgham for charges related to her peaceful participation in protests. Israa al-Ghomgham still faces a prison term, and Amnesty continues to campaign for her immediate and unconditional release.

March

In Ukraine, an International Women's Day rally organized by human rights defender Vitalina Koval in Uzhgorod, western

Ukraine, went ahead peacefully, with participants protected by police. The event marked a major change for the region, after similar rallies organised by Koval in previous years had been targeted by far-right groups, with police singularly failing to protect participants from violence.

AFRICOM admitted for the first time that its air strikes have killed or injured civilians in Somalia, after the release of Amnesty's investigation The Hidden US War in Somalia: Civilian Casualties from Air Strikes in Lower Shabelle. Following this report, US military documents came to light confirming that the US authorities knew of further allegations of civilian casualties resulting from many of their air strikes in Somalia.

Gulzar Duishenova had been championing disability rights in her country Kyrgyzstan for years. In March 2019, her persistence paid off when Kyrgyzstan finally signed up to the Disability Rights Convention. Amnesty supporters wrote nearly a quarter of a million messages backing her.

And in Iraq, just days after Amnesty and other NGOs raised the alarm about a draft cybercrime law that would seriously undermine freedom of expression there, the Iraqi parliament chose to withdraw the bill, confirming to Amnesty that its 'concerns have been heard'.

April

In April, love triumphed when a ban on all LGBTI events in Ankara, Turkey, was lifted by the administrative appeals court. 'This is a momentous day for LGBTI people in Turkey, and a huge victory for the LGBTI rights activists – love has won once again,' said Fotis Filippou, Campaigns Director for Europe at Amnesty International.

The District Court of The Hague issued an interim ruling in favour of Esther Kiobel and three other women who took on one of the world's biggest oil companies, Shell, in a fight for justice. Esther has pursued the company for more than 20 years over the role she says it played in the arbitrary execution of her husband in Nigeria. Amnesty has shared over 30,000 solidarity messages with Esther Kiobel, and is supporting her Kiobel vs Shell case in The Hague. As a result of this hearing, the court in October 2019 heard for the first time the accounts of individuals who accuse Shell of offering them bribes to give fake testimonies that led to the 'Ogoni Nine' – who included Esther Kiobel's husband – being sentenced to death and executed.

President of Equatorial Guinea, Teodoro Obiang Nguema, announced that his government would introduce legislation to abolish the death penalty.

May

Taiwan became the first in Asia to legalize same-sex marriage after passing an historic law on 17 May, with the first same-sex weddings taking place on 24 May. Together with LGBTI rights groups from Taiwan, Amnesty had campaigned for this outcome for many years. We are now working to end all discrimination against LGBTI people in Taiwan.

Qatar promised more reforms to its labour laws ahead of the 2022 World Cup. Human rights pressure also played a role in FIFA's decision to abandon plans to expand the 2022 Qatar World Cup to 48 teams, which would have involved adding new host countries in the region. Amnesty worked together with a coalition of NGOs, trade unions, fans and player groups, calling attention to the human rights risks of the expansion, including the plight of migrant workers building new infrastructure.

June

Climate change activist Greta Thunberg and the Fridays for Future movement of schoolchildren were honoured with Amnesty International's Ambassador of Conscience Award 2019. The Fridays for Future movement was started by Greta, a teenager from Sweden who in August 2018 decided to miss school every Friday and instead protest outside the Swedish parliament, until it took more serious action to tackle climate change.

In a long overdue move, Greece passed legislation to recognize that sex without consent is rape, and Denmark's government committed to doing the same. This development is testament to the persistence and bravery of survivors and campaigners for many years, and creates real momentum across Europe following Amnesty's 2018 review of outdated legislation in 31 European countries and other barriers to accessing justice for rape survivors.

From 1 June 2019, contraceptives and family planning clinic consultations became free of charge in Burkina Faso. The change was seen as a response to our 2015 My Body My Rights petition and human rights manifesto calling for these measures to be put in place. With financial barriers removed, women in Burkina Faso now have better access to birth control, and more choice over what happens to their bodies.

July

In a momentous and inspiring day for human rights campaigners, the UK parliament voted through a landmark bill on 22 July to legalize same sex marriage in Northern Ireland. The bill also forced the UK government to legislate for abortion reform in Northern Ireland, including decriminalization on the basis that a Northern Ireland Executive (government of NI) did not return in three months.

Also in July, in a US Congressional hearing, a senior Google executive gave the clearest confirmation yet that the company has 'terminated' Project Dragonfly, its secretive programme to develop a search engine that would facilitate the Chinese government's repressive surveillance and censorship of the internet. This followed Amnesty's

#DropDragonfly campaign, and hundreds of Google staff speaking out.

On 22 July, 70-year-old human rights defender and prominent Palestinian Bedouin leader Sheikh Sayyah Abu Mdeighim al-Turi was released from prison in Israel, after spending seven months in detention for his role in advocating for the protection of Bedouins' rights and land. Sheikh Sayyah thanked Amnesty International and all those who took action on his behalf: 'I thank you all very much for standing up for the right of my people and the protection of our land. While I was in prison, I felt and heard your support loud and clear, and it meant the world to me.'

August

Mauritanian blogger Mohamed Mkhaïtir, who was sentenced to death and held in arbitrary detention for more than five years after publishing a blog on caste discrimination, finally walked free.

In August, Saudi Arabia announced major reforms easing some of the major restrictions imposed on women under its repressive male guardianship system, including allowing them the right to obtain a passport which should make it possible for them to travel without permission from a male guardian. The changes also grant women in Saudi Arabia the right to register marriages, divorces, births and deaths and to obtain family records. While we welcome these changes, people campaigning for women's rights remain in prison, and we must do all we can to fight for their freedom.

September

Syrian national Ahmed H. was finally allowed to return home, after being imprisoned and then held in immigration detention in Hungary for more than four years. He had been arrested on terrorism charges after being caught up in clashes on the Hungarian border. At the time he was helping his elderly parents, who were escaping Syria and were crossing into Hungary as refugees. An amazing 24,000 people joined the #BringAhmedHome campaign, calling on Cyprus to allow Ahmed to return to his family.

A court in Tunis acquitted 18-year-old activist Maissa al-Oueslati, after she faced trumped-up charges that could have resulted in her imprisonment for up to four years. Maissa and her 16-year-old brother had been arbitrarily detained by police earlier in the month for filming a protester threatening to set himself on fire in front of a police station.

October

At midnight on Tuesday 22 October 2019, after a last-minute effort by the DUP to overturn the bill, same sex marriage became legal in Northern Ireland, while abortion was decriminalised. All criminal proceedings were dropped, including those against a mother who faced prosecution for buying her 15-year-old daughter abortion pills online.

Grainne Teggart, Amnesty International's Northern Ireland Campaign Manager, said it was the beginning of a new era for Northern Ireland, in which the nation was freed from oppressive laws that police people's bodies and healthcare.

'Finally, our human rights are being brought into the 21st century. This will end the suffering of so many people. We can now look forward to a more equal and compassionate future with our choices respected.'

November

Kurdish-Iranian award-winning journalist and refugee Behrouz Boochani arrived in New Zealand to attend a special WORD Christchurch event on a visitor's visa sponsored by Amnesty International. It was the first time Boochani, known for his work reporting on human rights abuses from within the Australian government's refugee detention centres, had set foot outside Papua New Guinea since he was detained on the country's Manus Island in 2014.

Humanitarian volunteer Dr Scott Warren was found not guilty by a court in Arizona of charges linked to helping migrants on the US-Mexico border. In a similar case, Pierre Mumber, a French mountain guide who gave hot tea and warm clothes to four West African asylum seekers in the Alps, and was acquitted of 'facilitating irregular entry'.

December

Alberto Fernández is inaugurated as President of Argentina on 10 December. As president-elect, Fernández announced he would push for the legalization of abortion as soon as he took office, saying: 'It is a public health issue that we must solve.'

The Philippines' Commission on Human Rights said that 47 major fossil fuel and carbon-polluting companies could be held accountable for violating the rights of its citizens for the damage caused by climate change. The landmark decision paves the way for further litigation, and even criminal investigations, that could see fossil fuel companies and other major polluters either forced to pay damages, or their officials sent to jail for harms linked to climate change.

The regional Economic Community of West African States' (ECOWAS) Court of Justice rejected a 2015 ban imposed by the government of Sierra Leone preventing pregnant girls from sitting exams and attending mainstream school – and ordered the policy to be revoked with immediate effect.

18 December 2019

The coronavirus pandemic threatens a crisis for human rights too

People could soon be arrested for a sweeping range of new offences, sparking troubling scenes in the UK.

By Afua Hirsch

You can learn a lot about someone's perspective from what they find reassuring at a time like this. This week I saw a private briefing from a bank, soothingly reassuring its clients that 'this feels more like 9/11 than 2008'. I think the point was to let investors know that this crisis is not systemic. It felt a bit like updating the old wartime spirit for today's hyper-capitalist economy: "Keep well-capitalised, and carry on."

I can think of a host of reasons why 9/11 does not bring calming thoughts to mind, but one is the long-term impact it had on human rights. Back then I was in the early stages of becoming a human rights lawyer. My very first day in court was with the team defending a victim of extraordinary rendition, where Britain had helped facilitate his torture. By the time I was practising, the 7 July London bombings had happened, and so had draconian new laws – 90-day detention without trial, plus sweeping surveillance and monitoring. Many Muslims remember this as the time that racial profiling and state harassment – in airports, on the tube, in the street – became the new normal.

This might sound like a strange issue to raise when the national priority is – understandably – how to stop the spread of coronavirus, treat the sick and tackle the hit to the economy. But since last month, when the government drafted emergency regulations to grant police new powers – and more far-reaching laws are expected this week – the potential has been building for a clash between liberty, privacy and public health measures. The authorities now have the power to arrest and detain someone they believe is infectious for up to 14 days, to move that person around from custody facilities including secure hospitals, and to take blood or saliva from them by force, even if they are a child.

The legislation set to come before parliament is likely to ban public gatherings, to widen police and immigration officer powers of detention and restraint, to give doctors powers to sign death certificates without seeing the deceased person's body, to allow fast-tracked burial and cremation, and to strip back services in care homes. People who refuse to self-isolate could be made to do so using the always contested 'reasonable force'.

Our human rights protections – long maligned by many of the politicians now running our pandemic-stricken nation – were designed for moments such as this. They contain specific exemptions for situations in which the state needs to contain the spread of infectious disease. And the continuing shutdown caused by coronavirus doesn't make them less relevant, it makes them more important than ever.

The proposed measures will contain safeguards – as they are constitutionally required to do so – especially rights to appeal. But this being a government that has decimated legal aid, brought our court system to its knees and repeatedly attacked the judiciary, a key element of trust is already compromised.

Trust is one of those ingredients in a democratic process that is hard to notice until it is gone. But this government's cavalier approach to applying the rule of law at the best of times – let's remember the prime minister misled the Queen and illegally prorogued parliament – does not inspire confidence at a time of crisis.

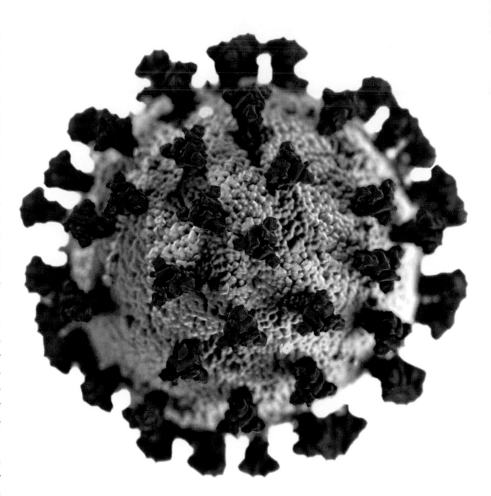

Lawyers who focus on the right to human dignity in the care of vulnerable or elderly people were appalled to hear Boris Johnson suggest that the deaths of vast numbers of British people would be an acceptable price to pay for so-called 'herd immunity'. One QC compared the idea to Germany's post-9/11 attempt to permit hijacked passenger planes to be shot down, as if the lives of those on board were expendable. Similarly, he suggests, the very idea of herd immunity would have 'subordinated human dignity by treating it as a quantifiable entity that can be measured and weighed in the balance'.

There's the potential for a kind of tyranny of the majority – one of the reasons we need human rights in the first place – and then there are the new, established but upgraded, tyrannies of the state. China has developed an app of remarkably intrusive proportions, using facial recognition to track both your movements and those of everyone in your proximity, so that they can be tested in the event you become infectious.

Israel is ditching superfluous apps altogether and simply allowing security services to hack infected people's phones to monitor their movements.

Donald Trump has insisted on a project of deliberate racial demonisation by calling Covid-19 the 'Chinese virus' – inflaming what we already know to be harmful prejudice against east Asian people, including those who have suffered shameful abuse in Britain. In one of the most surreal responses to the pandemic, commentators who are usually allergic to this form of social justice have belatedly discovered the concept of reparations – not for the genocidal abuses committed by Europeans over the centuries, but for Europeans from the allegedly guilty Chinese.

The truth is that China has been remarkably effective at stemming the spread of Covid- 19, but has done so through a heady concoction of human rights abuses and authoritarian rule, of which no one should be envious. Human Rights Watch has reported censorship; dissenters put 'under quarantine'; a disabled child left to die when his parent was forced into isolation; and a leukaemia sufferer turned away from hospital.

That doesn't justify racism against Chinese people any more than the British should be stigmatised for the uniquely dodgy leadership we currently endure. This pandemic has exposed what many of us said about the Tories' long boast of 'record high' numbers of people in employment – namely, insecure workers with no rights and no safety net. Likewise, we warned about starving the NHS so that its resilience is shot, creating a generation of renters with no savings, and allowing homelessness and destitution to mushroom.

These casualties had already become the new normal. But once we see newly troubling scenes – people arrested for resisting isolation or treatment – we will be reminded why this could become a crisis of rights, as much as it is one of disease.

19 March 2020

Key Facts

- The Universal Declaration of Human Rights was drafted in 1948. (page 1)

- Article 1 of the Universal Declaration of Human Rights: "All human beings are born free and equal in dignity and rights." (page 1)

- The European Convention on Human Rights was drawn up in 1950. (page 2)

- The United Nations Convention on the Rights of the Child ('the UNCRC') was introduced in 1989. (page 3)

- The Human Rights Act is a UK law passed in 1998. (page 4)

- Civil liberties are the rights and freedoms recognised by a particular country, that protect an individual from the state and which are underpinned by a country's legal system. (page 5)

- In 2000 the ECHR found that the UK had violated the human rights of several homosexual soldiers who had been dismissed from the armed forces because of their sexuality. (page 7)

- In 2010 the ECHR found that the stop and search procedures used by the UK police pursuant to the Terrorism Act 2000 were illegal because they did not require the police to have grounds for suspicion before using them. The ECHR found that this was open to abuse and constituted a breach of an individual's right to private and family life. (page 8)

- According to the latest report on forced labour by the ILO an estimated 40.3 million victims are trapped in modern-day slavery. (page 14)

- 71% of trafficking victims around the world are women and girls and 29% are men and boy. (page 15)

- 30.2 million victims (75%) are aged 18 or older, with the number of children under the age of 18 estimated at 10.1 million (25%). (page 15)

- There were 5,144 modern slavery offences recorded by the police in England and Wales in the year ending March 2019, an increase of 51% from the previous year. (page 16)

- The Modern Slavery Act for England and Wales was introduced in 2015. (page 17)

- In England and Wales, the most common offences recorded under modern slavery in the year ending March 2019 were 'Hold person in slavery or servitude' and 'Arrange or facilitate the travel of another person with a view to exploitation'. (page 18)

- Lungs, kidneys, livers, hearts and corneas are among the most sought-after organs and are sold on the black market around the world for thousands of pounds. Victims are often political prisoners or vulnerable, poor people. (page 21)

- Analysis of National Crime Agency (NCA) data reveals that in 2018, four children and two adults were among those who were flagged to authorities, having claimed that they were under threat of being killed for their organs. (page 21)

- According to the United Nations (UN), across the world at least 200 million women and girls are living with the impact of FGM. (page 23)

- The UN estimates 68 million more are at risk of undergoing the procedure before 2030. The majority are found across African countries including Somalia, Egypt, and Burkina Faso, as well as in Sri Lanka and Indonesia. (page 23)

- Since April 2015 there have been 21,510 newly recorded attendees (presenting with FGM) and 43,005 total attendances. The most recent data, from between April and June 2019, shows 2,905 total attendances by women and girls with FGM, of which 975 were newly recorded. (page 24)

- More than 250 million women alive today were married before their 15th birthday, many against their will. (page 27)

- 17% of the world's child brides live in Africa. (page 27)

- Child brides can be found in every region in the world, from the Middle East to Latin America, South Asia to Europe. It is a global problem. In the UK, the Home Office's Forced Marriage Unit supported over 1,400 suspected cases of forced child marriage in 2016. (page 27)

- Globally, 16 million girls aged between 15 and 19, and 1 million girls under the age of 15, give birth each year. (page 28)

- In 2019, Saudi women over 21 years old were finally given the right to travel abroad freely and obtain passports without permission from their male guardian. (page 30)

- Saudi Arabia executed 184 people in 2019, the highest number of killings since records began six years ago, according to human rights campaigners. (page 34)

- In a momentous and inspiring day for human rights campaigners, the UK parliament voted through a landmark bill on 22 July 2019 to legalize same sex marriage in Northern Ireland. (page 37)

Child marriage

Where children, often before they have reached puberty, are given or sold to be married – often to a person many years older.

Domestic servitude

A type of labour trafficking. Domestic workers perform household tasks such as child-care, cleaning, laundry and cooking.

European Convention on Human Rights

An international treaty that protects the human rights and freedoms of people in Europe.

Female genital mutilation (FGM)

FGM is a non-medical cultural practice that involves partially or totally removing a girl or woman's external genitalia.

Forced labour

When someone is forced to work, or provide services, against their will. This is often the result of a person being trafficked into another country and then having their passport withheld, or threats made against their family.

Forced marriage

A marriage that takes place without the consent of one or both parties. Forced marriage is not the same as an arranged marriage, which is organised by family or friends but which both parties freely enter into.

Human rights

The basic rights all human beings are entitled to, regardless of who they are, where they live or what they do. Concepts of human rights have been present throughout history, but our modern understanding of the term emerged as a response to the horrific events of the holocaust. While some human rights, such as the right not to be tortured, are absolute, others can be limited in certain circumstances: for example, someone can have their right to free expression limited if it is found they are guilty of inciting racial hatred.

Human Rights Act

The Human Rights Act is a written law (statute) passed in 1998 which is in force in England and Wales. The rights that are protected by this law are based on the articles of the European Convention on Human Rights. There is an ongoing debate between supporters of the Act and its critics as to whether it should be kept, or replaced with a new UK Bill of Rights.

Human trafficking

The transport and/or trade of people from one area to another, usually for the purpose of forcing them into labour or prostitution.

Organ harvesting

In relation to people trafficking, organ harvesting occurs when a person is trafficked into the country by people whose intention is to remove one or more of their organs and sell them on the black market.

Slavery

A slave is someone who is denied their freedom, forced to work without pay and considered to be literally someone else's property. Although slavery is officially banned internationally, there are an estimated 27 million slaves worldwide. Article 4 of the Universal Declaration of Human Rights states that 'No one shall be held in slavery or servitude; slavery and the slave trade shall be prohibited in all their forms'.

Torture

Intentionally causing a person physical or mental pain or suffering in order to obtain information or force them to make a confession. Under Article 5 of the Universal Declaration of Human Rights. 'No one shall be subjected to torture, or to cruel, inhuman or degrading treatment or punishment'.

United Nations Convention on the Rights of the Child (UNCRC)

An international human rights treaty that protects the rights of all children and young people under 18. The UK signed the convention on 19 April 1990 and ratified it on 16 December 1991. When a country ratifies the convention it agrees to do everything it can to implement it. Every country in the world has signed the convention except the USA and Somalia.

Universal Declaration of Human Rights

The first international, secular agreement on what were formally called 'the rights of man', which arose from the desire of the world's governments to prevent the recurrence of the atrocities of the Second World War by setting out a shared bill of rights for all peoples and all nations. The test is non-binding, but it retains its force as the primary authority on human rights, and has been supported by the UN's ongoing work to encourage its incorporation into domestic laws.

Activities

Brainstorming

◆ In small groups, brainstorm to find out what you know about human rights. Consider these questions:

· What are human rights? How many can you list?

· Is there a difference between human rights and civil liberties?

· What is the Human Rights Act (HRA)?

◆ In pairs, think about recent news events. Can you identify any major news stories where a breach of human rights law has taken place?

◆ What have been the biggest human rights issues facing the world in the last 20 years?

◆ What are the benefits of human rights and equality to your daily lives and communities?

◆ Write a list of famous human rights activists, past and present.

Research

◆ Using this book, and the Internet, research the issue of human trafficking and write a report about its prevalence in the UK.

◆ Read the article *Modern slavery in the UK: March 2020* (pages 16–18). What are the five main types of exploitation that victims of modern slavery may experience?

◆ What is the Palermo Protocol? What are the three aspects used to define human trafficking?

◆ Create a graph that illustrates the contents of the table on page 26. Think carefully about the kind of graph you need to use.

◆ Look up the European Convention of Human Rights (ECHR) and the United Nations Convention on the Rights of the Child (UNCRC). What do the laws and conventions of these acts do?

◆ Read the article *Child marriage* (pages 27–29). Where does child marriage happen? What are the causes and effects of child marriage? Produce an infograph to show your findings.

Design

◆ In small groups, choose one of the following issues and create a human rights campaign around it;

· Racial discrimination

· Gender inequality

· The death penalty.

Come up with a hashtag for your movement and design a leaflet with a small manifesto explaining the objectives of your campaign.

◆ Choose one of the articles in this book and create an illustration to accompany it.

◆ Design a poster aimed at raising awareness of human trafficking and forced labour. Include some statistics.

◆ Look at the article *A history of human rights in Britain* (pages 2–3) Create an illustrated timeline version of all the milestones listed.

Oral

◆ In pairs, create a PowerPoint presentation that explores the indicators of human trafficking. Include a section that advises people what they should do if they suspect someone has been trafficked.

◆ Divide the class into two halves. One half should argue for a British Bill of Rights, and the other half should argue against it.

◆ Choose one of the following articles from the European Convention of Human Rights (ECHR);

· Right to a fair trial

· Right to education

· Freedom of expression.

In pairs or small groups, discuss how your life might change if that right was taken away.

Reading/writing

◆ Write your own Bill of Rights for the UK. What rights do you think should be enshrined in law? Would all rights be absolute, or could some be limited in certain circumstances? What stipulations and provisos would you want to include with your list of rights?

◆ Read the book *Nineteen Eighty-Four* by George Orwell, set in a future dystopia in which the right to free expression is controlled by the nightmarish 'Big Brother'. Write a review. Do you think Orwell's vision is relevant to today's world?

◆ Read the article *In a dangerous world, human rights activists have been winning all year* (pages 35–38) Think about a human rights issue that is important to you and imagine you have campaigned for and won positive changes in the law regarding that issue. Write a newspaper headline and short article about your victory and how it will affect society.

Acknowledgements

The publisher is grateful for permission to reproduce the material in this book. While every care has been taken to trace and acknowledge copyright, the publisher tenders its apology for any accidental infringement or where copyright has proved untraceable. The publisher would be pleased to come to a suitable arrangement in any such case with the rightful owner.

The material reproduced in *ISSUES* books is provided as an educational resource only. The views, opinions and information contained within reprinted material in *ISSUES* books do not necessarily represent those of Independence Educational Publishers and its employees.

Images

Cover image courtesy of iStock. All other images courtesy of Pixabay, Rawpixel and Unsplash.

Icons

Icons on pages 9, 10, 14 & 15 were made by Freepik and smashicons from www.flaticon.com.

Illustrations

Don Hatcher: pages 8 & 33. Simon Kneebone: pages 16 & 36. Angelo Madrid: pages 3 & 12.

Additional acknowledgements

With thanks to the Independence team: Shelley Baldry, Danielle Lobban, Jackie Staines and Jan Sunderland.

Tracy Biram

Cambridge, May 2020